MEMORIES OF AFRICA

EVENTS EXPERIENCED IN SOUTHERN AFRICA

By

Robert Mazibuko

RoseDog ❧ Books

PITTSBURGH, PENNSYLVANIA 15238

RoseDog Books
585 Alpha Drive
Suite 103
Pittsburgh, PA 15238
Visit our website at *www.rosedogbookstore.com*

ISBN: 978-1-64957-888-4
eISBN: 978-1-64957-909-6

DEDICATION

This book is written at the request of Ronald and Grace Fudu of Port Elizabeth, South Africa, and is dedicated to all the pioneers who came to teach the Baha'i Faith in Southern Africa. Particularly remembered are those whose dust lies buried under the soil of the continent of Africa. Ronald and Grace made the observation that , in the book *This Side Up*, not enough is mentioned of the immediate day to day Baha'i activities, and felt that such involvement should be specifically explained, as many were other participants in the story. This was gratefully welcomed.

PREFACE

This is a story of a few events experienced in teaching the Baha'i Faith in Africa, especially in the Southern region of that continent. Parts of such a story cannot be adequately told since the eye cannot see itself except in a reflection. Others may find reason to tell the story differently. Here the writer tries to capture a sequence of events as he remembers them. Thus the pictures he uses are linked to time and place and are an impetus to search the mind and establish reason as well as the circumstances attending each event. In that sense, this is not a researched work, rather it is events remembered, before the mind fades and thus render those who exist in the future, unable to grasp the impact of the past on their times.

The author grew up in the Cape Province of South Africa and was a witness as Port Elizabeth grew from a handful of Baha'is in the African townships, in 1957, into a local community encompassing the whole of Port Elizabeth; from the time when a few stalwart friends assisted in building a Baha'i Community that embraced many parts in the region of Southern Africa, encouraged by souls who decided to spend most of their lives teaching in that land, some of whose bodies lie buried in the soil of the continent of Africa...

This stories told are , therefore, is not limited to the events in the Eastern Cape but take in what the writer experienced as he began to grow as a member of a world community.. Eastern Cape has to be the starting point, as the writer himself first became conscious f the Baha'i Faith while residing in that part of the world.

Knowledge of some persons mentioned in the stories, is obtainable from the following sources:

Tending the Garden, (Ilona Sala Weinstein, White Mountain Publishing, Canada, 1998);

Volumes of *The Star of the West (Vol. 12 p. 33; vol. 20 p 321, 337; vol. 22 p. 5, , p 1, p. 4, p. 25)* as well as *Volumes of Baha'i World (Vol. XVII, Vol. XX* and *The Baha'i World 2000, 2001* (Baha'i World Centre, Haifa, Israel), unde*r In Memoriam);*

An unpublished story written by Emeric Sala;

Heroes and Heroines of the ten Year Crusade in Southern Africa, compiled by Edith Johnson and Lowell Johnson (National Spiritual Assembly of the Baha'is of South Africa, 2003).

Brief stories of first pioneers who came to Southern Africa are also in the book *A Pictorial History of the Baha'i Faith in South Africa 1911-1992* (Johnson L.; Ford S. and Goodman, P, 1992.).

Otherwise. Some facts were obtained first hand from experiences with the pioneers and African believers. In *The Star of the West,* Emeric Sala's first name may appear as Emerit, Esmeric or as Emeric.

The pictures used are either taken by the author or those taken by others who were in his company. Some pictures are gifts from other Baha'is, as specified and a few are from documented sources.

THE EARLY DAYS WITH
ROSEMARY AND EMERIC SALA

THE BEGINNINGS

 A starting point for understanding the growth of the Baha'i Faith in the Cape Midlands is the time of the coming of the Salas' to Port Elizabeth and the work rendered by Rosemary Sala at a school in New Brighton..

NEW BRIGHTON AND COWAN IN THE FIFTIES

Vincent Ludumo Qunta

In order to have a picture of the circumstances that pertained at Cowan and in New Brighton Townships at the time of the arrival of Rosemary Sala, one has to have insights into the kind of person Vincent Qunta, the principal at Cowan Secondary School, was and why his wife decided to become a Baha'i at an early stage, a stance she soon gave up.

Vincent had been a political activist in the past. I have heard my friend Stanlake Kukama(a member of the Baha'i National Spiritual Assembly of South Africa in the late seventies, who lived in a Tswana-speaking area), a Ba-

3

ha'i who had himself been involved in political activity, mention him in that connection, even though they were from different parts of the country and different African cultures. Stanlake would often ask me about the wellbeing of Vincent with much concern and pleasure.

Vincent was a strict disciplinarian, an attitude which pleased many parents in New Brighton and Walmer (a township on the other side of town), immensely. In his time at Cowan I only heard of one pregnancy occurring among the students, and that after graduation.

Vincent was an athlete as well as the girls' netball trainer. His hobby was hunting, and for that he owned a number of hunting dogs, some of which were pure breeds. He owned cows which he had milked every morning, and he sold milk and *sour milk* at his home. He often so regaled students with tales of his hunting exploits, for, no teacher we knew in the township was interested in hunting. This pastime had been given up by adults and left to young boys..Very few older men hunted; all worked in the city.

He was the senior class Latin Teacher and took great pains in introducing students to an understanding of the culture Romans and Ancient History. At one stage he invited the whole school to go and watch the movie *Hannibal*. A story of a general, who attempted to capture Rome with a team of elephants, taking the unusual path of crossing the Alps.

In his home there existed two religious denominations prevailing, Catholic and Protestant.

For his school and school children he wished the best. He chose the motto of *Nil Nisi Optimum* (Nothing but the best, is good enough). He wished this attitude to be upheld by both students and teachers and was respected, and feared in some cases.

Despite that, he was kind and empathized or sympathized with students as the situation required. Yet none dared to speak without some respect with him

Vincent wanted progress for the students but there was no such progress under the prevalent regime, for *Bantu Education* was already in place and the understanding of students concerning the world was limited. Bantu Education was a system by which African children were taught in all schools, only of certain issues about the world, and those to a very narrow extent. Vincent publicly wept on announcing that even university education was going to change that year, under this system.. We had very little of an idea as to what this event entailed except that we had been taught at lower standards to accept instruction in Xhosa and not in English. How this was going to apply at university, we could only learn from our teachers. For the time being, however, at junior high instruction was undertaken n English.

The coming of Rosemary Sala, therefore, signalized the approach to a window outside the country for both teachers and students alike, for Rosemary was Canadian and would have innovations and attitudes from outside the country.

As a politically inclined person, Vincent was attached to ideologies of freeing Africans and this was part of his agenda. He found the teachings of the Baha'i Faith on Unity of Mankind attractive, but could not find reconciliation between that and not taking part in political activity. His wife, Grace, joined the Baha'i Faith for a while but found herself unable to express herself academically because, in those days, even the Africans who were Baha'is took the Baha'i Faith to be just another "church". This was not satisfying to academics, even when several Baha'is attempted to explain the universality of the Baha'i World Order. Soon she left the Faith.

THE POLITICAL ENVIRONMENT

This was a period following World War II. Much hunger and distress had been caused in the townships by that war, but the advent of the rule of *apartheid* did nothing to make the load any easier to bear. Besides the coming of reference books and the Group Areas Act, Bantu Education for all Blacks had been instituted. Not only that, but that Influx Control was playing havoc on families, no one, not even students could live in the city without the correct permit. In short there was a disruption in the schools because of frequent riots. By the time, the few got to junior high ,many children had left school in support of political strikes. Subjects taught in junior high were limited in scope and named differently from what had been before. For an example, there was to be no class of Physics and Chemistry, the class was called *General Science;* there was going to be no class called Geography or History, both would go under *Social Studies,* A new class called *Afrikaans* was introduced and teachers from the Northern Provinces were imported to teach in our schools, because in the northern parts of the country, there was a larger Afrikaans-speaking population. This was the main language of the race that governed at the time.

It became painfully clear that we were going to study different content from the students before us. In high school we would not study for the Cape Senior Certificate but for the Certificate of *the Joint Matriculation Board.* In derision students called this JMB , "Just Meant for Bantus". Even though students were not aware of the true meaning of Bantu Education, it was becoming clearer with the passing of time, especially knowing that the Minister of Education had made a statement that he wanted to "put the Kaffir in his place." This statement was quoted in a newspaper, to our alarm. Nevertheless, the coming of Rosemary Sala balanced things for teachers and students, for here was a white lady wishing to work in a school under a black principal. This passed the message that there were some good people somewhere.

Because of the situation that pertained, any person or student who left to study or stay overseas was cheered. Some of our teachers left for free African states and for overseas destinations. This exodus was to increase as the government hounded some teachers and increased the strictness of its race discrimination laws. Those who remained knew hey had to find ways of improving the quality of education in some way. For example, some teachers gave instruction of what to expect at university level, for at the time, university methods had not deteriorated to a greater extent as was the case later. These were initial stages and the past behaviors still persisted among students.. However, disaster struck even in that quarter. Sorrow descended on the school when it was announced that the only university where Blacks were accepted had been placed under an Afrikaner university as a college and removed from an English speaking university to which it had been affiliated for years. This was a time of hidden and overt discontent; as was evidenced by the rise of political organizations and resultant frequent strikes, as awareness of conditions grew..

THE SALAS IN PORT ELIZABETH

A partial picture of the house Emeric and Rosemary Sala occupied in Canada before moving to Africa (Picture taken in 2005)

By now we all know why the Salas came to Port Elizabeth, their main aims and purposes were well defined. They had left Canada in order to teach the Baha'i Faith in Africa. What is not known is the impact the Salas had on Port Elizabeth, more specifically, on Cowan Secondary.

By the time Rosemary and Emeric moved to Africa, having both served in Canada on the first Baha'i National Spiritual Assembly of Canada, Emeric had already written a book, and delivered many papers on diverse subject all dealing with subjects on the teachings of the Baha'i Faith.

Rosemary Sala

The coming of Rosemary Sala to Cowan was a time of excitement. The school was going to be associated with the outside world. Several overseas visitors began to stop by and see the school. In this way Rosemary and her different attitude were more of a ray of sunlight in a dark room than just the arrival of another teacher. Her willingness to work with the teachers as one of them endeared her to all. It was also a joy to hear the teachers address her as "Rosemary" and speak of her as "Mrs Sala" when referring to her in the presence of students. In reality, Rosemary's name had been 'Mary' until she found out that in her Baha'i community in Canada there many persons by that name. Of a necessity she opted to change her name to 'Rosemary'. Rosemary was accepted by both the principal of the school as well as by a notoriously strict Inspector of Schools, Ormond. She was to operate as the volunteer School Librarian.

To beautify the school, Vincent had built a rockery in the foreground and included successful flower beds. This attempt pleased Rosemary greatly. .Every year the school would have Rosemary and Emeric Sala as definite honored visitors at the School Prize-Giving occasion. Soon they both contributed to this effort by including the *Sala Shield*, which was to be given, with a sum of money, to a student who showed high positive qualities. There was also a Library Prize form the Salas'. Sometimes Rosemary would split prizes among students so that no one student took all the prizes. This was the case amongst library helpers. The library prize was given to a different student each year. This was reasonable, as there were four students who were library helpers in all.

THE LIBRARY

Having been introduced at Cowan, as a volunteer librarian by a lady called MS Van Hattam, who was herself a volunteer librarian at Newell High school, New Brighton, Rosemary was assigned a room at Cowan secondary, where she could start a library for the school.

The room which was to be devoted to library work and the housing of books, was very small and was being used by teachers as a *staff room*. Therefore, the library had to be shared by students and teachers. Certain days were designated to be library days when students could exchange and borrow books. This was a cheerful time for students as they could visit the beautiful library, instead of sitting at desks.

When the Inspector of Schools approved the installation of new shelves for books in the library, the Librarian and her helpers knew that they had won. We were permitted to have a school library and Rosemary could stay in the school.

Rosemary decorated the library with pot plants and collages of pictures of interest to the students. When the room assigned proved too small to accommodate all the books, the library was soon moved into a larger area where two classrooms had the wall separating them taken down to form the library, Eventually, years after the Salas' had left South Africa, a library was built and opened in a different area. A plaque with Rosemary's name placed at the door. The event of the pacing of the plaque occurred after Rosemary had passed on in Mexico. Next to the library was built a Computer Room with some rows of Personal Computers.

A group of students at Cowan
(Picture taken by Rosemary near 1959)

As the library grew, so did the number of students who visited each day of the week, when Rosemary came. On her arrival, the principal would instruct students to help her with bringing books in. This was another joyous moments for students, because, not only did Rosemary bring books from far away lands, but she also brought musical records and clothing. She called the clothing "samples", though they appeared new and sealed in packets.

Students in the library at Cowan High (From personal collection)

Nozizwe Mdodana, principal at Cowan in 2004, who never ceased to mention the part played by Rosemary in empowering lady teachers in the schools of the African townships (Picture taken by author in 2004)

Two teachers in the Computer Room adjoining the Library. They permitted me to talk to students on the subject of computer programming(Picture taken by author in 2004)

EMERIC SALA

Emeric Sala was born in Hungary and his actual name was derived from Emereich Salavich . His name , Emeric, means "valiant" He explained this when I named my son after him. This name had been common among people in his area. On reaching Canada, Emeric had abbreviated his name to Emeric Sala, in he same way that my African name is Kholekile, and yet it is not registered on my documents except in the documents of the Baha'i Faith.

While Rosemary started work at Cowan, Emeric, on the other had established a business in soft goods (Sala & Co.) at Alliance Building, Strand Street in the city. His help in advising Rosemary was invaluable because, Rosemary would not embark on any enterprise without first consulting Emeric whom she respected .Emeric had been a great spokesman in Canada and an author of many papers on Baha'i subjects. One of his works in the book called *This Earth One Country,* He was known to be fluent in many languages, including French, German and Spanish. His ability to use his expertise was limited at that time. Subjects on international topics that might sound political were prohibited amongst the Baha'is in those early, dangerous years of the Faith in

South Africa. What religious people wanted to hear, was a drawing away from such topics and a dwelling on more spiritual attitudes. There was a limited attitude that any subject which dealt with internationalism was political, in the same way that the government regarded any challenge of its policies as being communistic. Such a situation could occur only in South Africa! Albeit, there was a need for a broader understanding of religion than, song, dance and good behavior, to be pursued on both sides. Good behavior has to be the result of some values one had overtaken. There is much more to religion that can be expressed. For example, the meaning of its tenets and its teaching about what life is, are huge subjects. At this time, such attitudes were not accepted as being part of worship. Religion has to stand the test of reason, logic and science, and must address needs of the body politic.

Emeric was an honest man who believed in rewarding hard work and encouraged his workers to excel in good qualities. All his workers were given the opportunity to be co-partners in his company, but none would accept such an offer. It was unknown and unusual to the workers.

Each prize giving day, he and Rosemary and Emeric would turn up with prizes for students. Emeric supplied all the samples to be given to students by Rosemary.

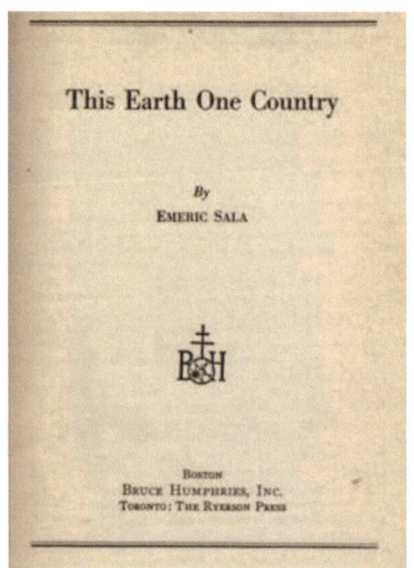

A book written by Emeric Sala while residing in Canada

ROSEMARY AND EMERIC AT HOME

I met Rosemary and Emeric when they lived at 12 Selwyn Court , Summerstrand, an apartment near the beach. They had very simple furniture and an old phonogram on which Rosemary would sometimes play the Handel's Messiah. They had few musical records but gave a lot to the students, even rock 'n roll music. Emeric was vegetarian and once in a while partake of chicken. They were both great readers and passed some of the books they had read to me. Once Rosemary loaned me a book called *The Psychology of Dreams Visions and Reflections* by Jung, which of course I lost to someone else who borrowed it without returning. Some books they read were the whodunitst hat I loved in my youth.

Rosemary loved cooking for visitors and would sometimes invited multiracial guests to one table. These were the only times it was possible to cause Emeric to speak his mind. Otherwise, he kept his silence. The reasons are explained in he book *This Side Up* (Mazibuko, 2010)

After South Africa, the Salas' moved to Canada , but soon left that country to pioneer in Mexico. One of the reasons they chose to retire was a desire to be someplace where they could not have the advantages enjoyed by Whites in South Africa and which the Blacks could not.

Emeric Sala at table, possibly during a lunch break

13

On her last day in this world, while residing in Mexico, Rosemary cooked one of the best dishes for Emeric After going to bed Emeric woke up and felt uneasy about Rosemary in the night. On waking her up he found that there was a serious problem. Rosemary had passed on(This account is given later by Emeric Sala). They knew some Baha'is who were doctors and Rosemary had just written me marveling at the construction of the human body that is attached to a soul.

THE APARTMENT

Selwyn Court where Emeric and Rosemary lived
from 1957 to 1968. The beach was visible from their balcony.

From this apartment Rosemary launched her many projects: appeal for books from overseas, main libraries and consulates; parceled up food and clothing for the poor and destitute ; planned agendas for students who wanted to progress educationally and above all, organized teaching plans for the Baha'i Faith. Cutting and pasting of collages and mounted pictures , were also done here , as well as the patching, covering and cataloguing of books for the libraries of Cowan High, Newell High, and Kwazakhele High schools , among others. Most of the work was done in a room she termed *The Horrors*. This room contained miscellaneous items that Rosemary kept for her projects. In one corner of the room, hidden behind a curtain, were some books belonging to Rosemary's Baha'i Library. I found these quite by accident one day.

When the library helpers were in the apartment chatting with Rosemary while working on books, they would be asked to pause at lunch, go to her bathroom, wash hands and join her and Emeric at lunch. At school she would bring a thermos flask of a cold beverage and some sandwiches. This made me feel like a child who was doted upon.

TEACHING THE BAHA'I FAITH

Teaching the Baha'i Faith was undertaken in peril of being accused of communistic tendencies. This has been dealt with in the earlier book called *This Side Up* by the same author.

Fred Gqola,
Robert Magaqa
and Diesel Mpame

When I became a Baha'i in 1962 , I met six African Baha'is: Frederick and Winnifred Gqola; Diesel and Caroline Mpame and Robert and Eunice Magaqa. All lived in Kwazakhele. I joined the Faith on the same weekend my friend Pitso Mafata joined. However, by 1967 I was the only African Baha'i remaining. It is to be noted that, just before the Salas' left, two ladies declared their faith. One was a school principal Dzingwe and the other a hospital sister who worked at the local clinic, Nomvula Sotomela. These two were to be of assistance at a later stage.

CONSULTATION, BUSINESS AND MOUNTAIN CLIMBING

Emeric and Rosemary consulted together on all matters but on most of my weekend visits to the apartment, Emeric would be away on mountain climbing in the Hogsback Mountains. In this way I got room to talk openly to Rosemary and, we as library helpers had the apartment to ourselves. Also, Emeric could channel word through Rosemary and not mention the Faith himself. This worked fine. However , on some days I was invited to dine with Emeric and Rosemary, and this would break Emeric's silence. He certainly could not avoid conversation when he would come on his lunch break to enjoy it with me and Rosemary. I would giggle on some evenings when he would come home and would go straight to he pantry to crunch nuts before dinner. Whenever I made an observation that Rosemary liked she would have me repeat it to Emeric when he came from work. Emeric was the first to notice that I too did not care for meat n those days, and for the next seven years after that I was also a vegetarian and did not like even chicken.

I declared my Faith in front of Rosemary and Emeric in heir apartment and Emeric told me that he wished I could teach the Faith until all of Africa cried "Ya Baha'ul' Abha!"(O Thou the Glory of the Most Glorious).

ROSEMARY BANNED

.Many times I had to deliver sums of money and packages to different families about whom even I knew very little. She would knew their condition and helped according to each need. Some of the families she helped had relatives in jail for political activity and some were actually involved in political activity. One has to remember that Baha'u'llah says: we should be defenders of "the victim of oppression"(*Epistle to the Son of the Wolf*, p. 93)..Eventually she was banned by the government from entering African townships. However, most of those whom Rosemary also helped were students from destitute homes, and she had no knowledge of their involvement in political activity. It is easy to mention one's name when one thinks that person is not really involved and this may have happened to Rosemary. When her banning order had come, she took me aside and informed me. After three years as a French teacher in a Colored school, she and Emeric consulted and Emeric felt the inspiration that they both should leave the country perhaps pioneer somewhere. Initially they left for Canada, their home.

THE "KITTY" CALLED A "JACK"

This story was funny only to me. Sometime before the Salas left South Africa, I found nine five Rand notes in the street. To me this was a great opportunity to buy a farewell present for Rosemary and Emeric. I went to some trouble asking Emeric what he wanted for a present and he said he wanted a "kitty". He further explained that a kitty was also called a "jack". He saw that I did not comprehend his meaning and explained that a kitty was a round ball used in bowling! I had never played nor witnessed a match in bowling , even though in my college there had been a term and activity called "bowling" when you had to aim for a goal. This had nothing to do with a ball but had to do with hitting a good mark when making an impression with one of the opposite sex.

This kind of ball was hard to find in the city. It took me all day, waling up Main Street, from North End to South End, to find a sports shop that sold "kittys", but I finally found one and it cost me no more that three Rands. It helped to have Emeric write down the name because I found myself feeling ridiculous asking for a "kitty"! in a sports shop. He probably knew I was going to find this difficult. This was the only time Emeric ever asked for anything of me, except to encourage me to teach the Faith, and it happened to be parting present. He had said that, in future, every time he used the ball he would re-member the parting. The evidence is as follows:

A note written by Emeric Sala

I felt so childish walking down Main Street in the City Center looking for that, but I found it! . The only bowling we knew was in cricket!

Caroline Mpame in the balcony of the apartment at the Salas'
(Picture taken possibly by Rosemary)

EmericSala outdoors

The Salas lived in Port Elizabeth and introduced the Faith to teachers, social workers , students and general workers from 1957 until they left for Canada in 1968.

While Rosemary was the first to pass on in Mexico where they later pioneered, Emeric passed on later in Canada where he had gone to see doctors because of a medical complaint he had..It is poignant that before they had thought of leaving for Mexico, I had referred to them as *mamacita* and *papacita*, a situation they loved.

THE PASSING ON OF EMERIC SALA.

Emeric Sala passed on the 5th of September,, the birthday of Emeric Mazibuko, my eldest son. On the 23rd of that month my mother also passed on. The 23rd happened to be the anniversary of my declaration as a Baha'i. In that year two people who were important to me passed on. I heard of Emeric's death after the 6th September when Ilona Weinstein, his niece, called me with the announcement.

Emeric had moved back to Canada in order to be near doctors as he was unwell in Mexico. He wrote to give me his address in Victoria in British Columbia. I did not hear fro him for a long while, and, therefore called his brother , Ernest who lived in the Montreal area. I was very surprised to hear that Emeric was at Ernest's home at that very moment. I spoke to Emeric Sala for the last, at that time. He assured me that he would take good care of himself.

After the passing of Emeric , I received a recording of the funeral service from his other brother Paul, who also lived in Canada..

I later heard the story that Emeric had had a health condition which necessitated surgery. The operation was done but he never recovered. I was , in a way glad I had spoken to him before he left. It helped to know that, one of the people present at the funeral was the Secretary of the National Assembly whom I had met in Israel in 1978.

The agonizing pain of this loss in 1990 ,left me with a situation of depression by 1991; perhaps because I held my tears at the time of the passing and did not cry enough about that.

EXCERPTS FROM A LETTER FROM EMERIC

This is a note written by Emeric after the passing on of Rosemary:

"Guadalajara, Feb. 26, 1980
About Rosemary's last days on earth to her closest friends.

She was cheerful to the end, and I was confident to have her precious company for several years. She was looking forward to our trip to the coast, which we had been planning for weeks. While we were in Manzanillo from Jan. 21st to 24th, she enjoyed our walks meals and the rest…

What caused her greatest joy and satisfaction was locating and visiting Baha'is in Manzanillo , particularly Senora Celia Muniz de Macias , the last Baha'i friend Rosemary has spoken to, with whom we had enjoyable lunch on Jan. 23rd. The next day , our last day together, we returned in rain and fog…

After six hours of driving we arrived home to a cold house, with electricity out of order. We lighted our gas heater and gas light. At seven, Rosemary went to bed wither supper , to keep warm, and read by flashlight. At ten when I went to say good-night, she asked me to join her…When I was about to fall asleep, as we were close to each other, she said:"I feel I am getting par-alyzed. These were her last words. Half asleep I retorted out of empathy: "So am I. Let us pray." After praying I fell asleep.

Early in the morning I felt something was wrong….

Seventeen cables arrived, three from Haifa; from Toronto, Africa, St. Lambert, Barbados, Oshawa, Vancouver, Rawdon, Point Calire, Yukon, Chomedie , Willowdale ,,New York and Montreal. Beautiful flowers from 200 Baha'is gathered at a Que-bec Regional Convention . And many letters and telephone calls, all assuring fervent prayers…She remained unconscious for twenty seven days….

Rosemary had several premonitions which I ignored .One

of her greatest joys these last years , were the preparation of Albums for the Shrine in Montreal. While working on an album last month, she said,' this is my last one'. She also said that she was getting old and tired. She was 78.In Manzanillo she said, without context,' my Baha'i work in Mexico is coming to an end'... Rosemary served the Faith unstintingly for fifty two years. We travelled together about a million miles, in about seventy countries on four continents, mostly in the interests of our Faith.

Latterly Rosemary closed many of her letters :' With deepest love until we meet again in this world or the next.' Now e can meet her only in the next world.

Emeric"

SOME FRIENDS OF THE SALAS'

Edwin "Koko" and Eunice Fikiswa (Magongo) Kabi and their daughter. Rosemary practically brought up Fikiswa, as a library helper. Both had been students at Cowan. (Picture possibly a gift to Rosemary and was received from Ilona Weinstein in 2005)

Julia Tabina (Ntsuka) Galo ,
a retired nurse and wife of the Science Teacher at Cowan High
(gift from Ilona Weinstein)

Rosemary had friends in rural Transkei. The two were possibly school teachers.
Once I found one of her scrapbooks in Cofimvaba, Transkei.
The handwriting on the scrapbook told me it was one of Rosemary's.
(gift from Ilona Weinstein)

MY FRIEND AND I

*Ferdinand "Pitso" Mafata and
his wife Lorna Mafata.
(a gift from Rosemary Sala)*

Pitso and I became Baha'is on the same weekend of the 22nd / 23rd September, 1962. He left Port Elizabeth to become an actor practicing at *Dorkay House* in Johannesburg. Pitso, subsequently left South Africa and settled in New York, United States. He has just been to South Africa after about forty years he left.

STATE OF AFFAIRS WITH MEETINGS

The early days in South Africa, that is the fifties and the sixties, were immediately after the Nationalist party came into power. After the setting into place of the Pass laws which affected every African, there followed the Group Areas Act, which designated places of residence for all races in the country; the Riotous Assemblies act, which prohibited the meeting together of more that ten Africans, except for schooling and religious observance occasions. These were more markedly enforced during periods known as the State of Emergency, when soldiers would patrol the streets of the townships. Of these the Pass Laws made it possible for any African to be stopped and searched by the police, to determine whether he or she had a Reference Book at hand. Some of these laws were enacted under the statement of the Suppression of Communism Act, which had possibilities of tagging any form of objection as communistic. In the latter environment, all foreigners almost always fell suspect.

There were businesses run by Whites in the New Brighton Townships, but all these Whites were usually Jewish. Such businesses ranged from soft goods, groceries, entertainment and Medial activities. It is tragic that , during the rioting that soon ensued, the first Whites to suffer losses , both of property and life, were the Jews in the townships. This happened because they were viewed as Whites capitalizing on the Africans and not as sympathizers with the situation.

Under these unrelenting conditions, the first Baha'is wished to have multiracial interaction with the Blacks. The result of these stringent conditions made it necessary for the first Baha'i meetings to be furtive and apprehensive. However, contact was made first in the schools, with the 'master servant' relationship being sometimes a cloak for meetings. This meant that, if the police turned up, Africans took up positions of employment, while the Whites supervised, until it was safe to continue a meeting. Thus , it became possible for Rosemary to have Library Helpers in her home from the school she volunteered to work in.

Baha'i meetings had to be held mostly in the evenings , if all were to attend. Arrival at the venue had to be with care, with no group of Africans arriving at the same time or from the same direction. The entrance would have to be the back of the home, in the White Area.

Under these conditions, Rosemary and Emeric ,managed to establish a group of Baha'is first in Kwazakhele, to later spread to the rest of the townships, in due course. Regardless of that, establishing any thing new in any area is usually hard to do, how much more difficult would it be to establish something that appeared different from the cultural scene? But the Salas relied on real assistance from God. I have hear Rosemary say :"I drove through the townships, whispering the Greatest Name over and over again!" No wonder that when I declared as a Baha'i, Emeric voiced is wish of :"You must teach the Faith until all Africa cries out Ya Baha'ul Abha!"

AFTER THE DEPARTURE OF EMERIC AND ROSEMARY SALA

CHANGES CREATE POSSIBILITIES

 The sixties, saw the changing of South Africa to the Republic of South Africa; the changing of the monetary system into decimalization, as well as the first inklings of establishment of Homelands for Africans. By the late 70s, some of the Homelands were created, and it became possible to hold multiracial meeting in those sub-countries. In the mideighties, the Immorality Act which prohibited marriage between people of black and while colors, was repealed. Open meetings of Baha'is were still watched but, gradually this was being relaxed. Perhaps because of pressure, Africans could stay in five-star hotels with some ease. The road to this situation was long, arduous and full of many dangers. Others may, at some time , find it necessary to recount some of the general and specifics of these times from the point of view of individuals. Here mostly the stories about Baha'is are told. Needles to say that I personally have had friends either die in jail or during interrogations by government officials.

The Baha'i events that immediately followed the departure of the Salas, saw the formal introduction of the Faith to the authorities, and occurred at a time when the government administration was engaged in the establishment of homelands. Thus there much division of thought as to what was good for the Africans and what was not. Some of my friends felt that it was very well to accept bread, so long as one was certain that it was bread, in fact. In other words, was what the government offering in the homelands enough to satisfy every African?

WHEN EMERIC AND ROSEMARY LEFT SOUTH AFRICA

At this time, there were no more than three Baha'is in New Brighton and one in Kwazakhele, but we had many African contacts who were friends of the Salas.

After the Salas left, I started to translate some of the Baha'i Writings into Xhosa, having accepted advice from Betty Randall, another United States pioneer, to make the effort in that direction.. I was subsequently appointed a travelling teacher of the Baha'i Faith.(This story is told in the book *In Spite of All Barriers*, by the same author.

When in 1969 I went travel-teaching with Lowell Johnson, I had had occasion to speak to the township authorities in Port Elizabeth about holding a public Baha'i meeting in New Brighton, where Blacks and Whites could attend. On the strength of the agreement of the administration we knew we stood a chance of being recognized in the town, at least. Indeed, later in the early eighties we had no difficulty in holding a multiracial National Teaching Conference in the town ship. This story is told in the book *In Spite of All Barriers* (Mazibuko, 2011)

ACTIVITIES IN THE COLORED AREA

In 1968, 1970 to 1972, I worked in a glass factory with some Colored Machine Operators. One of them , William Benjamin heard of the Baha'i Faith and joined. This offered a great opportunity, because in the Colored area, mixed meetings were permitted, whereas in the African townships they were not. This meant that we could entertain international company at their home. The Operator's brother Bernard, a Carpenter, soon declared and he and his wife Delores permitted me to visit on Sunday mornings.

William "Billy" Benjamin, the first Colored Baha'i in Port Elizabeth. (gift from William Benjamin)

SOME OF THE PEOPLE WHO VISITED THE BENJAMINS'

John Agulhas
a Musician from Cape Town

Lowell Johnson in Johannesburg
originally from USA

Dr Michael Walker,
originally Australian

We held many meetings at the Benjamins' and sometimes with Baha'is from out of town, who could not enter the African townships.

*Jacques and Susan Von Frasukieviecz and family
from U.S.A., now settled in Brazil*

One Sunday morning I visited the friends in the Colored area to deepen on the *Kitab-i-Iqan*. We had just got started when there was a knock at the door. The visitors were a White man and a woman with a child. We were surprised and I immediately thought it was perhaps the police. The man announced that he knew Dr Mike Walker of Cape Town. It was with great relief that we settled down to a friendly conversation. The man explained that they were new pioneers who had come from the United States.

BREAKING THE NEWS

Up to this point, I had never been able to talk about the Baha'i Faith in my home. I lived with both my parents, but refrained to say any word on the subject of religion, My parents attended the Anglican Church and I was the only Baha'i. There were no grown or younger people I could refer anyone in my family to, and I knew that the subject was not welcome.

After the National Convention of 1972, I acquired pictures of the Shrines that are on Mt Carmel in Haifa, Israel, had them properly framed by an expert, and displayed them in the room I slept in, next to my bed. I had a present of a framed picture of 'Abdu'l-Baha which I had been given by Rosemary before she left South Africa. That picture was propped up on my desk, near the door of the room. No one, not even my mother commented on the setup. It is obvious that I longed to have a home of my own where I would be free to behave as I saw fit.

I was visiting in East London, when I was told that the son of Esther Nkonzo was a serious Baha'i. I noted this casually as I had not yet met him.

One morning, while I sat pottering around the room, I was told I had a visitor. It was Theophilus Nkonzo, the son of Esther. He was quite open in introducing himself as a Baha'i to my mother and the family. He further introduced himself as a clan of Radebe, which was my maternal grandmother's clan. This meant that Theo was my relative and could be allowed a closer look on the family. These two categories opened the door to a more amenable atmosphere in my home. Theophilus requested to come into my room. Having been granted permission by my mother , he entered and was astounded to find all the pictures I had on the walls. I felt that I had made a profitable move by procuring the pictures and framing them.

On asking about his business in Port Elizabeth, he said he had come to see his wife who was nursing at the local hospital. He pointed out that it would help if I came along.

We were successful in meeting with his wife and spending time with her. I could have screamed with joy , because, at my home, I could now speak of the Baha'i Faith openly and without any unpleasant looks being directed at me, thus stifling all conversation in that area. From that day, my religion was recognized as being the Baha'i Faith and that I had relatives worshipping with me!

*(R)Theophilus Mbulele Nkonzo,
at the front of the hospital with
Robert Mazibuko*

QUESTIONS TO GRAPPLE WITH

During his first visits in the colored area, Michael introduced himself as a teacher in a school in Cape Town. However, conversation made it impossible to keep his profession a private. Actually, when I met Michael in 1969, he already held a PhD in Mathematics. In other words he was a scientist. He was perhaps about twenty nine years when we met and was teaching in a university. It was possible to forget this when chatting on Baha'i subjects with him.

One day Bernard Benjamin had a question for us and he directed at Michael: Why was it that all Scientist did not care for religion? Michael gently assured him that some scientists did believe in God and religion. Bernard insisted that, anywhere one found scientist one would also find that they did not care about any religious belief. Michael then looked straight at Bernard and said:"But Bernard, I am a scientist!" That jolted Bernard into silence for a moment.

MARVEL GRAY AND LANGUAGES.

Marvel was from the United States but by the time she came to South Africa she also spoke Portuguese, having learned that language in South America. In order to acclimatize herself to the environment in which she then found herself, she learned some Xhosa. I must say she did quite a good job at that. Once or twice she would write in that language. Here is an except from such a letter which I later translate:

"22/9/70
Botha Robert!

Allah'u'Abha! Usaphila ke? Ndisaphila kakhulu. Ndilusizi andikub-halelali kodwa ndisebenza kakhulu Bekukho inkomfa e-Caledon iCawa, 6 September. AbabaBaha'i

baseKapa, baseBredasdorp nabase Caledon bapheleke. Bekukho 65 abantu nabantwana 50…

Warmest Baha'i love to you and all the friends,

Marvel"

(A brief translation would be " Are you well then? I am also very well. There was a conference in Caledon. Baha'is from Cape Town, Bredasdorp and Caledon attended. There were 65 people and 50 children participating.").

Marvel soon moved to Angola where she taught in Portuguese until it was inadvisable for her to stay there any longer than she had done. These were the troubled times of the seventies and the eighties in that part of the world.

MICHAEL WALKER AND TEACHING

Some five years after his arrival, I perceived that Mike understood French and some Spanish. In the country he was in he had learned both Xhosa and Afrikaans. This latter language came in handy in the teaching work since all of the Colored population spoke that language. I realized the importance of this knowledge not only in translations, but when we had to deal with government officials or helping to drafting documents of incorporation. He understood most of what was law in South Africa at that time.

The improvements he brought to translating both in Xhosa and Afrikaans were inestimable, because he also understood the tenets of his Faith.

On learning of my translating activities , he advised me to use the King James version of the Bible as well as the Xhosa Bible, as this would work well in using terminology from those sources. He explained that the Baha'i Writings were translated to English by the Guardian using such terms. To help in this endeavor, he purchased a Concordance to the English Bible, which was of great use. He had a number of Xhosa Dictionaries which he passed on to me in the course of translating years.

Soon Mike was appointed to the Literature Committee which has to oversee all translations of the Holy Text into local languages. Later he was to be appointed to the Baha'i Publishing Trust of South Africa when it came into existence.

RONALD FUDU, THE WILLING MAN

Ronald and I shared a commonality: we were not of good health , at the time, but we were both willing to work together in service to the Cause of Baha'u'llah. What made him stand out was that he had an enquiring mind and was willing to stretch out a hand in friendship with other races in the country. He became one of the first active Baha'i in the town ships and the first to attend deepening classes at our home in Hopa Street. When it came to travel-teaching he undertook a project with enthusiasm. Once he had to attend a summer school in cape Town ,but on his way had to call on another town, Mossel Bay, to do some teaching. Although not accustomed to the town or its people, he achieved this project with such diligence that we remained close friends with that community for many a year. It, therefore did not surprise me when his son married across culture and all his children achieved college degrees.

Nevertheless, Ronald is no stranger to himself or his culture. In his email to me he always addresses in the usual way, the simplest Xhosa with lots of humor, as if we still lived next door to each other. Such people keep one buoyed up even in the midst of misery.

Ronald or "Fudu", as he is called, and his wife, Grace, keep African cultural laws their own special way which has become appreciated by both the Whites in the country as well as new visitors. Someone has even produced a video program on this family and placed it on the Internet.

THEMBU AND IVY GCUME

Another couple who impressed me with their candor and love of justice was the family of the Gcumes'. They became the backbone of children's classes in the area of Zwide. To help identify themselves with the Faith, their two children are named Bahiyyih and Bayan, names that are known in Baha'i History very well. With both of them, things had to be run according to the rule every time. Deviation after the law was known was not acceptable. In entering the Faith, they brought most of their family in Somerset East into the Faith and so enriched the membership to a great measure. This also gave opportunity to expand into Cradock and the Northern parts of the Cape Province. Xhosas love a law and order, and Mthembu and Ivy both subscribe to such an attitude. I could not agree more, for the fabric of the Faith depends on respect to the law of the Faith and living the life of a Baha'i. Today Bayan serves at the Baha'i World Center.

ASSEMBLIES IN PORT ELIZABETH

After the travel teaching with Lowell Johnson in 1969-70, two Local Spiritual Assemblies were formed: In New Brighton and Kwazakhele. Both Assemblies would form at election each year, would elect office bearers by plurality vote, but would not function after that.

Correspondence from Lowell, Mike Walker and Marvel Gray gave a great boost to the teaching work.

In the years between 1972 to 1974 , I had just started to attend National Conventions and National Conferences each year.

ONE PERSIAN PIONEER ARRIVES

The first time that I heard of Sadri's presence in the Cape, was when Dr Michael Walker called to ask if "Mr Farabi" had arrived yet. I did not now the last name, but I knew a Mr Farraby who was a Hand of the Cause and had write the book *All Things Made New*. I naturally thought the latter was the correct spelling of the name. I answered that I had not heard of any Farabis in the area. He then asked me to call Rhodes University and inquire of him in the Department of Economics.

I called Rhodes and spoke to a number of persons in Economics and Registration, and could not locate any Farabi as a student. I called Michael and informed him of my failure to find him. Mike then later called the university, and could not find him , until one professor exclaimed :" Oh, you men the Arab man!". That is ho we located Sadri at Rhodes University.

I soon learned from Sadri that he was from an area in Iran where they spoke both Arabic and Farsi well. In glossary of the Kitab-i-Iqan , "Sadrih " is defined as '"branch". He was doing a Master's in Economics but was cut off from funds from his family. So, in order to earn a living, he visited auctions and bought all manner of house items, repaired them and sold them to the students. I found , in his digs at Grahamstown's Anglo African street, a shy unassuming man who was devoted to the Faith. Somehow, I earned his confidence, and he would take me into confidence about many personal issues, and I would try to advise in accordance with the culture of the area. He took such advice seriously.

Anglo African Street became the contact location for the Baha'is of Zwide and many meetings and conferences were held at that address in Sadri's room. Sadri lived there from about 1974 until his death in late 1981 or early 1982. I know he was there when I married in 1980 and gave me his well-wishes. As presents, he gave me many house utensils , and asked me to use my wife's nickname that I gave her, sparingly as it could mean the opposite to 'wonderful'. The nickname was "Badi" as her name was Nomabhadi. He gave this advice in his quiet amused way, and I thought very little of it until much later.

As a result of Sadri's stay in Grahamston and the assistance of the Baha'is of Zwide, Port Elizabeth, the two localities of Fingo Village and Joza

Township were opened to the Faith. Fingo Village even attained Local Assembly status. My wife was from those areas. Sadri was encouragement to all and was the first Persian we ever knew in Port Elizabeth. His presence at out Unit Conventions and teaching meetings in Port Elizabeth brought a good flavor of the international with it and made our belief more of a reality.

Sadri was buried in Grahamstown and has the one grave with the Greatest Name on it. Every time the friends have to travel to Mdantsane, they have to pass Grahamstown as it is only 80 miles from Port Elizabeth. There are buses and trains there and pirate taxis travel everyday. I know the road well as I once bicycled there over twelve hours with pauses. I feel that Sadri is still a presence in that area.

Sadri Farabi at the beach in Cape Town during a break at summer school.

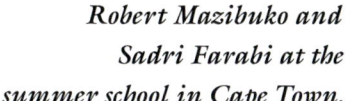

Robert Mazibuko and Sadri Farabi at the summer school in Cape Town.

(L-R)
(Front)Robert Mazibuko, Faith Mazibuko, Bernard Benjamin.

(L-R)
(Back) Sadri Farabi, Ronald Fudu and Peter Simon, at the home of Bernard and Dolores Benjamin.

MEMORIES OF MDANTSANE

MDANTSANE

Mdantsane was a little township outside East London in the early sixties. It had been part of moving residents out of the townships of Zipunzana and Kwatsolo, which deemed no longer habitable. Very few people wanted to move, but some, my uncle being one of them, saw this as an opportunity to invest in a house. One could buy a house or rent it in Mdantsane.I had briefly visited the township of Mdantsane for the first time in 1972. In that same year, Michael Walker made arrangements for a teaching trip to the Eastern Cape. As before, I would stay at my aunt's home in Mdantsane.

On that first visit, we met with Rose gates at her home. I found that George Gates had a great respect for Michael as a professor in a university, however Mike kept pulling me into the conversation, until it was understood, by George, at least, that I had to be spoken to as part of the general company. This was a quiet morning before we drove into Mdantsane for the meeting with the friends.

From Rose, I learned that she had started teaching at the hotel, meeting there many of the African ladies who were assisting visitors, and eventually inviting some to her room. Rose had obtained papers of residence in South Africa in order to teach the Baha'i Faith.

To me , Mdatsnae seemed very subdued an hollow, with hilly surroundings. There were not that many people in the streets but I met one person, at least who used to live in New Brighton, Port Elizabeth. The township was composed of persons from many areas around the country. I suspected that it was the government's dumping zone. The name of the town seemed meaningless if not insulting to an extent, but here the Faith was to blossom into a lovely flower. They say that the lotus flower will blossom, notwithstanding the filth in the river. I eventually loved Mdantsane, even though it was the first township in which I was attacked and robbed at night.

This attack occurred when I was heading home, on a Sunday night, after a weekend with the friends. I was in god spirits and humming to myself in the dark. Mdantsane was not properly lit in those days. Suddenly, I was hit on the head with what felt like an iron bar. I was searched by two young men and my watch was removed. As they were attempting to hold me down and hit me for the second time, I became more conscious, fought back and scrambled to my feet. My bag of best travelling clothing was taken, as I removed myself hastily, from the scene. I hurried to my aunt's home where my cousin who is a nurse, helped and rushed me to the hospital as I was bleeding from a wound on the temple of my head. I was subsequently referred to a hospital in Port Elizabeth, with the doctor exclaiming just how close I had been to death, had I been hit a few centimeters in the wrong direction.

I, however, continued visiting Mdantsane in the same way, after this event, and using the same route but not at night. Mdantsane became a scene of some great Baha'i activities.

THE IMMEDIATE IMPACT OF ACTIVITIES IN MDANTSANE

The event of renewed activity in Port Elizabeth was due to the arrival of Rose Gates in East London and the transfer of residence of Faith Kato from Mdantsane to Port Elizabeth.

Rose came and transformed the lives of many Africans in Mdanstane such that their lives were never the same. Faith Kato and her aunt, Beauty Kato, were the first Baha'is in East London. Their lives were touched by the spirit of the Cause of Baha'u'llah and they became very effective teachers. There is no one they knew whom they did not tell of the Faith. When I married Faith in 1973, she moved to Port Elizabeth. Through Beauty and Faith the Faith spread to Mdantsnae, Faith's home town of Keiskammahoek and so to St Matthew's.. As Faith was so young and enthusiastic, with a lot of determination, she won the hearts of the youth of our neighborhood in New Brighton. Many young people joined the Faith through her. She was appointed to the National Youth Committee by the National Spiritual Assembly.

Rose Perkal-Gates (extreme left) at the House of Worship, IL. Rose was a pioneer in South Africa, from the United States, from 1969 until she left in 1985. (Her story is in Volume 2000-2001 of The Baha'i World, p. 270)

THE SUMMER SCHOOL IN LESOTHO

Faith Kato (Mazibuko) at the Benjamins' in 1974.

While we were visiting in Mdantsane , Rose announced that there was going to be a summer school in Maseru, and encouraged all to go. It was 1973 and Ronald had just declared. The three of us, Faith, Ronald and I decided to find the money and transportation to go to Lesotho. Passports were applied for successfully..

Ronald Fudu in 1976. Ronald was my co-worker when he declared in 1972.

The two Counselors who were present at the Summer School: Counselor Bahiyyih Winckler and Counselor Shidan Fat'e'azam, emphasized to the youth the importance of this Day and the importance of living the life of a Baha'i and teaching the Baha'i Faith. This generated new enthusiasm on even the adults who were present. It was a solemn moment when the Baha'i Center in Maseru was being opened to use on that occasion. This was a new Baha'i Center. Iran Sohaili from the National Assembly of Zimbabwe, chanted a beautiful prayer for the dedication of the Center.

The summer school in Lesotho in 1973 cemented a lifelong relationship amongst us in far away Port Elizabeth and gave us courage to strive to build a community of Baha'is around us.

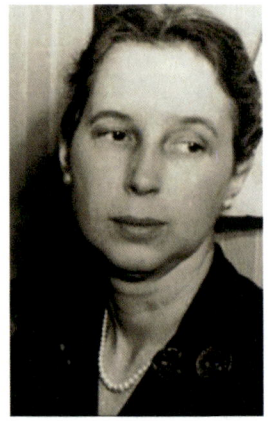

Counselor Bahiyyih Winckler (Picture from Bahai Gallery Website)

Counselor Shidan Fat'e'azam (Taken by author on a bus from Tel Aviv to Haifa in 1978 during the Baha'i International Convention)

AFTER THE SUMMER SCHOOL OF 1973

ACTIVITIES AT HOPA STREET, NEW BRIGHTON

Faith Nonyati (Kato, Mazibuko)
and young Emeric at Hopa Street

THE YOUTH AND THE BRAAIVLEIS AND GROWTH

 On returning from the summer school, we invited the youth and children in the area of New Brighton to a *braaivleis*, which is a version of a barbecue in South Africa. The year was about 1976 and my first son had been born. Faith was employed at the meat Counter at a Super Market and meat was available at reasonable prices. She therefore purchased some kilograms of it and brought it home. I appreciated this because I had just started eating meat again, after travels with Lowell. Lowell felt that being vegetarian was making me sensitive and gave the message that others would have to give up meat in order to be Baha'is, an erroneous notion.

A group od youth and children
at the barbecue

Our group began to grow when Eric Madikane and his girlfriend, Zukiswa Ximiya joined us. To add , Wisdom Mboyi, whose sister, Grace, Ronald eventually married got interested. Wisdom and Ronald worked with me at Lennon's Laboratories, and declared at our employment. Eric joined the same company and we got acquainted. Zukiswa was Eric's girlfriend and she joined after him.

Ronald, Faith, Zukiswaa, Eric and Emeric

NEW PIONEERS ARRIVE

Kris Amadeo, a pioneer from the United States.

Kristine Amadeo and Steve Burgess pioneered for a while in Port Elizabeth. Most of the time, they observed how the local Baha'is conducted teaching, because they were then new pioneers in the country and were getting accustomed to their surroundings. Soon they moved out to another post but were well remembered..

I was elected to the National Spiritual Assembly, at this point.

NATIONAL ASSEMBLY MEETINGS

A *DEFINED ROUTE*

 My being elected to the National Assembly occurred in 1975, just before Patrick and Christine moved to Port Elizabeth. The election immediately posed a question: How was I going to negotiate going to Johannesburg for meetings. Granted I was given the airfare to reach Johannesburg, but who was I going to stay with, if I consider that I wanted to do this with least assistance. I thought of my uncle in Soweto, but what time would I reach Soweto: 11p.m. on a Friday night is not a god time for a stranger to arrive. I became more positive as I undertook to plan the journey. When I adopted the plan, I would keep to it for years.

First, I found out if anyone was available to pick me up from the Rotunda in Johannesburg, the air terminal in the city. The Counselor Daniel Ramoroesi agreed to pick me up. A ticket was bought from the travel agent via the telephone, and delivered to the company Receptionist, who would then call me to collect it; then I sent two telegrams, on the week I departed from Port Elizabeth; one telegram was to announce to my uncle that I would arrive and specify only the date, the second was to Daniel specifying the date, flight , and time of arrival at the airport , so that he could estimate the time of my arrival at he Rotunda by looking up the terminal bus time table.

An announcement to the head of my department had to be made to the effect that I was not available for overtime that weekend.

Early on that Friday I picked up a borrowed small travelling bag with travelling sundries in it , and a small briefcase I had, together with my lunch box and headed for work.

At the end of the working day, I boarded a bus to the city. In the city I would go to the Post Office and call a taxi to the airport from the call-box next to the Post Office, incidentally, this was also next to a Police Station. On the plane I kept my briefcase under my seat and the bag on the rack. I was always assigned a seat at the back of the cabin, but that did not matter , for I needed my silence in keeping to my plan and schedule.

The flight took one hour and a half, if direct, and more time if it went via East London, and travelled roughly between 7:30 p.m. and 10:00 p.m. At he Johannesburg Airport, I rushed through the hall to find a bus at the exit. The bus would leave at about 10:30 p.m. and arrive at the Rotunda in about 30 minutes. If I were not picked up, I would have had to catch a train to Phefeni Station, as I did catch the train once or twice. Daniel who lived in Meadowlands within Soweto would meet me with a friendly, understanding smile , and drive me to my uncle's pace. At my uncle's home it was "Friday night"! But, I would find my place to sleep ready, even if on a mattress on the floor. I enjoyed moments watching the scene of dancing in their living-room, before turning in.

Early the next morning I would have to be awake by, at least 6:00 a.m. in order to catch a train at about 7:00 a.m. Arriving at Park Station, in the city, I would exit the same way I had been taught in 1969, and end up on Harrison Street. I would walk down Harrison to Bree Street. Some four or so blocks from Harrison is a bus station. I would always take the Ferndale bus, which dropped me off near 23 Rustenburg Road, where stood the Baha'i Center. There were several other buses which went past the Melville/Mill Park area, for an example the Randburg and the Honeydew buses but Ferndale was more reliable and never failed me. On Saturday nights, Ephens Senne who was on the Assembly, would drive me to my uncle's and pick me up the next morning.

This routine was adhered to until the Assembly thought it too dangerous and difficult. The change became that, from the Rotunda I had to call a taxi which would take me to Holiday Inn where I would stay until Sunday morning. A trick I learned at the Holiday Inn was to avoid booking for the continental breakfast but opt for the British breakfast!

The trip home was easier. Usually one of the pioneers would take all those leaving for the airport to the bus at the Rotunda. From there on everything was taken care of until arrival in Port Elizabeth. In the Port Elizabeth city I had to rush for the 10:30 p.m. bus which was the last bus. I never missed it even once!

THE SYSTEM FAILS

My system and route of travel failed only once. I was to travel on Friday night to Johannesburg, however, the flight from Port Elizabeth was canceled because of bad weather. I was then booked to travel on a Saturday morning. The next morning I discovered that I had been placed in the first class seats instead of the economy class which was cheaper. The difference of the ticket price had to be paid and I needed to be on the airplane. I called my employer at his home, and fortunately he lived near the airport. He drove to the airport with the money in and even enquired if I needed any more than I asked for from him. I appreciated that very much. Though I was late by a day, I was able to attend the meeting at the Baha'i Center.

MAX IS WAITING

After moving out of Soweto, and before being housed at the Holiday Inn by the Assembly, I was assigned room at the Seepes'. It became Max Seepe's task to pick me up from the Rotunda and take me to his home at Western Township, each Friday night that the Assembly met.

Max and May Seepe went to much trouble preparing for my visit, even to the extent of placing a hot-water bottle between the sheets of my bed to take away the chill in winter.Johannesburg was cold in winter! This very welcome situation pertained for several years until he Assembly decided that there was a need that all visitors be housed in an area which was not only safe but makes every member of the Assembly accessible for any emergency meetings.

Max was a retired teacher and an ex chauffeur and told me of his many exploits as an insurance agent, in which capacity he functioned when I met him. Like many Africans who lived in Johannesburg, he often told of sad stories of Sophia Town and treatment of Africans as they attempted to cross the area. Max had a sense of humor and often snickered in laughter as he told some of his stories.

May Seepe, Max's wife , on the other hand was a concerned mother, who always waited for my arrival at nearly midnight, with joy. With her would often be her granddaughter, Courtney, who was perhaps of kindergarten age at the time. Arrival was a moment of great felicity, as if it were a family reunion. Courtney was good-mannered and would not sleep without coming out to bid me goodnight each time I came. I remember her well at breakfast table the next morning when she would split bacon into little bits and then pick the bits up, one by one with her fork.

I got to know Max very well as we were sometimes placed in the same area in hotel when the members of the Assembly traveled to different lands or towns.

SWALLOW THE PILL

Soon after I was elected to the Assembly, somewhere between 1975 and 78, the National Spiritual felt the need to be closer to the believers. The Assembly decided that we would not meet at the Baha'i Center, as we usually did, but would instead meet in different towns. Meetings were held in East London, Durban and Cape Town. At the time of this story, the members were on a international flight to Windhoek, where a meeting was to be held. At this time, I was prone to tension headaches and had to take muscle relaxants. On the flight to Windhoek, the air stewards and hostesses, though using English also spoke German and were not, to my thinking used to South Africa. As usual I took asked for a glass of water from the air hostess and took two pills. In swallowing them I choked very badly, to the consternation of everybody. Michael Sears got up from his seat and gently banged my back to dislodge the pills. When everything settled down, I felt so embarrassed, but Mike looked at me with humor and said:" You are supposed to swallow the pill, not breathe it in!" We both laughed and so did everybody.

MEAT, RARE?

There were lots of funny moments though most of the time it was all seriousness during Assembly meetings. During the weekend session, we would sometimes go out to eat on Saturday night, and reconvened later. At this time Rose and Joyce Dwashu were on the Assembly. Michael Sears took the task of paying for the meal that Saturday and invited the members to a steakhouse. Lowell and I chose a vegetarian diet while among others, Joyce, like an African would, chose a steak-meal. However, there were complications, for the waiter wanted to know how each one wanted the steak. Perhaps Joyce was distracted, for she chose that a meat be not hard cooked. The waiter put that down for rare. When the meal came, Joyce declared that she could not partake of the meat, because it was too bloody. Africans do not eat their met bloody! It has to be well-cooked. The meat was re-cooked and returned. In later years I met with an African girl in the United States. In conversation she said:" Do you notice something about meals in the United States?" Surprised, I said :"What?" She said:" Everywhere I am invited for a meal, there have to be lots of leaves on the table!"

RELATIONS ON THE ASSEMBLY

It was not easy to be on the National Assembly, because one had to deal with issues which did not naturally occur in one's life, but the Assembly members were always a happy crowd. The membership of the Assembly changed many times over the years, but the believers on the Assembly always remained one and all servants of the Institution. What the Assembly wished it would cause the consultation to decide upon. The Assembly is not the members and the members are not the Assembly. This is the spiritual visualization of a Baha'i Assembly, local , national or international.

The Assembly members were not rigid in attending to business, in the sense of keeping to the agenda. The Assembly could take up personal matters involving one or the other of its members; settle that, before proceeding with the agenda. It was always a loving relationship of friends. There were no misters on the Assembly, but a Hand of the Cause or a member of the "House" was always introduced as Mister, but that was dropped in consultation but no respectfulness was omitted when addressing that member. As servants of the believers, Assembly members, as a habit and need of honor, would all stand up when a member of the community entered the consulting chamber, for the purpose of consultation on any matter. It was curious that Mike Sears referred to Lowell as "LJ" while Lowell called him just "Mike".

*Lowell Johnson
and Michael Sears*

Elise Liknaitzky

On the other hand , Elize Liknaitzky was always meticulous in the use of business terms. Phrases like *a propos of; In lieu of* would often be used by her as Treasurer of the Assembly, at that same time she was kind and endearing when addressing others in her soft-spoken voice.. Another member who was wont to use some meeting terms was Cornelius Khunou. Whenever a point he wanted to raise was dealt with by another member, he would say *: my point is covered.* At some stage while I was on the Assembly as the only Xhosa-speaking member, but regaled the Tswana-speaking Khunou and Kukama with a Tswana song I had learned while working in a construction company. The first lines of the song were*: Mangoane ntsoarele kefositse*...It had the two friends tickled, during the lunch break. I also learned not to say "tickled to death", for there is an occasion when one can be tickled to death, literally!

Nevertheless, there were moments of great joy, moments of great concern and moments of deep grief, depending on what had occurred in the Baha'i

World. Before all decisions and at such moments, prayer had to be turned to, to ask for assistance from the Concourse on High, whom we believed would oversee each meeting.

(L-R) Cassiem Davids, Elise Likniatzky and Maureen Page in the consultation room (1968). (a gift from Maureen)

THE TIMES OF THE BEERS

THE BEERS ARRIVE FROM THE JOHANNESBURG AREA

 In 1976 a family of pioneers, the Beers came to settle in Port Elizabeth and it became a reality to form an Area Teaching Committee of the Cape Midlands as differentiated from the Area Teaching Committee of the Eastern Cape. The area that included Port Elizabeth stretched now to the surrounding towns of Grahamstown, Mossel Bay, Cradock and Somerset East. The Baha'i friends were travelling to these towns almost every weekend. It so happened that the Baha'is in Port Elizabeth had relatives in many towns both in the Cape Midlands and Eastern Cape..

The story of how an Assembly was formed in Zwide, Port Eliabeth is told in *This Side UP* (Mazibuko, 2010).. It is worthy of note that after my family left Zwide, Ronald Fudu, Thembu Gcume, Ivy Gcume and Grace Fudu remained active Baha'i figures in that vicinity.

Patrick and Christine Beer

Patrick and Christine Beer came from the United Kingdom to pioneer in South Africa. Patrick who worked for the I.B.M. Company started off as a Statistics Officer for the community of South Africa. After a Convention they attended the family decided to move to Port Elizabeth. In Port Elizabeth they moved into a suburb, Mill Park, where there were no Baha'is, but in a secluded area. This enabled them to meet with African Baha'is in their house in a measure of privacy. Prior to their stay in this area, no African had visited any house in Mil Park, as a plain visitor. All Africans came in as servants or to perform some task related to their employment.

During this time, Baha'is had to abandon everyday or weekly habits and be prepared to move from work to some destination where they could teach the Faith. This behavior was imperative because it occurred many times that Patrick would make an appointment to come from his job and pick up a group of Africans from their place of employment and drive them out of town to teach for a weekend. There was relentlessness about the way they taught and insisted that the friends should be deepened. Of course this left some unable to cope with new methods, as they were used to being left alone to stay in the townships, when away from work. However, wishing to deepen the Baha'is who had the capacity was not viewed with any favor among some of the friends as they felt left out. This did not discourage the growth of the Faith. The Beers insisted that the Baha'is should behave as Baha'is in their own way and not mimic any one group. In such an environment, the usual activities of Africans in the township were taken into account and approved, so long as they broke no law of the Faith or government.

It is during this time that community life in the African area began to take root. The Beers regarded themselves as an integral part of the Baha'i community in the townships and were willing to give advice on any behaviors. It was a revelation to hear them talk about some of the disadvantages of a few Baha'is in their previous communities overseas. The Africans felt related to such experiences. The Beers got involved in personal matters. When there was a functioning Assembly as well as an appointed Area Teaching Committee they could not be regarded to have left their post without guidance when they had to return to the United Kingdom sometime in 1979. It was harder for them to intervene in matters that the Assembly could handle. When they left a spirit of courage to function and independence to choose had been born among the friends. The Beers' were missed by all as having championed the cause of forming a community with all the ramifications of Baha'i activities.

TRAVELLING TEACHING

This was a time of extensive travel in the Cape Midlands and the Eastern Cape. Besides the Beers' car we had one old car amongst us , and it belonged to Reginald Mcebisi Vimbi. Reginald offered to use his car any where or at any time we needed it. He was also our driver when we rented kombis to take us on longer trips to, perhaps Conventions, as we did once .Later Tembu Gcume who with Ivy, his wife opened the Somerset East area to the Faith, bought another car to help. However, by the time Ronald bought his, he was the only one with a useable car during that one later period.

In the Eastern Cape, Rose covered an extensive area in the greater then Ciskei. Many villages and towns were opened to the Faith in this way. Proper statistics would give a better picture, but there are very few towns in the Eastern Cape which were not visited either by Rose herself or the travelling teachers.

Robert and Angelinah Gcum (Cnter) in Mossel Bay during one of the trips arranged by the Area Teaching Committee. Patrick Beer drove them over for a weekend of teaching.

THE FOUR TEACHERS FROM THE UNITED KINGDOM

At the time when the community of Zwide was beginning to stir, four young teachers arrived from the Uited Kingdom. At this time only their teaching and first names are remembered. They were Abbas, Novin , Gita and Zarin. As they were passing through on travel teaching, we met them at the home of the Beers in Mill Park. We were amazed that such young people like ourselves found time to visit communities in Africa. That evening assured us that we were on the right track, as our community was composed of mainly young people. It was truly an enjoyable evening. It was plain that these young people came to meet with us because they could be introduced by the Beers who knew them from their homeland. How grateful we were that we could be so fortunate as to be noticed!

MEETINGS IN PORT ELIZABETH

Initially many meetings in Port Elizabeth were held in homes or schools(some at Ms Dzingwe's school, Charles Duna Primary) , but later it became possible to hold some larger meetings in a hotel called the *Alabama Hotel* which was in the Colored area. This allowed for multiracial mixing. At this hotel, we were offered the use of the *Blue Room* each time.

A unit convention at the Alabama Hotel where Patrick Beer and Sadri Farabi attended with the African and Colored Friends

THE SUMMER SCHOOLS IN CAPE TOWN

By 1975 I was no longer concentrating on visiting Mdantsane, as I did before, and there were then many willing good travelling teachers covering even rural Eastern Cape.

The National Assembly of South Africa, in encouraging all Baha'is to recognize themselves as Baha'is and help them take their religion more seriously, decided to hold summer schools in December, from around the middle of that month to the beginning of the new year. Many Baha'is traveled from the Eastern Cape, Durban and Gauteng, to Cape Town to meet with old friends and listen to talks. It was a happy time of learning.

HAND OF THE CAUSE JOHN ROBARTS

At one of the first of these summer schools, Hand of the Cause John Robarts and his wife Audrey, were invited. Hand of the Cause Robarts gave talks for an hour daily for a week. His main subject was the *Baha'i Daily Obligatory Prayers* :how to say them and what spiritual effect they have. This became a realization of some of the attitudes one has to adopt as a Baha'i.

Audrey Robarts gave words of encouragement to the author when he confessed to his inability to handle the subject of The *World Order of Baha'u'llah* that he had been assigned. She promised that, with practice one can improve. The one joy and consolation was that Audrey brought with her a note which she had written at the hotel to give to me:

A NOTE FROM AUDREY ROBARTS:

"Feb.-8-81
Johannesburg
Dear Robert,

Emeric's brother asked me to deliver this to you when I arrived here. Since I do not know when or when we shall meet I am leaving it in Lowell's care as he will probably see you in the near future…..

We wish you well.
May God's love surround you.

Sincerely,
Audrey Robarts.

Audrey also gave me a picture of the bedroom of Baha'u'llah taken from an image on a mirror.

Hand of the Cause John Robarts

Summer School at the Cape Town Baha'i Center with Hand of the Cause John Robarts(center), and Rose Gates in a red coat.

At one of these summer schools, Patrick Beer had to deliver a talk on the *Kitab-i-Iqan*. I shall not forget that in his talk he mentioned that when one becomes a Baha'i, all past transgressions are forgiven but after that he or she becomes accountable.

SEARCH FOR A BAHA'I FRIEND

Although this is a story about searching for a friend, it is really a story of meeting two dogs on the road. From childhood, I never got along too well with dogs. I knew two things about dogs: they scare you by barking and they bite when they catch you in the street as you passed the house of the owner on errands.

There was a Baha'i who had trained me in how to perform an interment of a Baha'i in 1969, and, since arrival in Cape Town, I had not seen him at any of the sessions. His name was Khaniff..On inquiring from his friends, I was given his address.

One morning before sunrise and before classes begun at the summer school; I went in search of my friend. As I neared the address, I saw two large black dogs. As I approached , the dogs growled. I had stopped and started backing away when both dogs came bounding at me at speed. As they neared me, I speeded up backing away. In doing so, I stumbled and fell backwards, hitting the road with both palms of my hands. To my surprise, the dogs turned and left! Someone came out of one of the apartments and called out to the dogs. I continued on my trip but had unfortunately injured both my wrists.

I was to deliver a talk that morning. Though I remembered everything I had to say in the talk, I had the added tasks of bandaging my wrists with the accompanying pain..

MARENGHEZ MUNSIFF

The year following that, we had Mrs Marenghez Munsiff from the United Kingdom; attend our summer school as an invited guest. She gave talks on spirituality and prayer. During her talk she told a story about herself and prayer.

She was home and feeling dejected somewhat. She said a prayer and decided to write to an old friend, after the prayer. Sometime later, she received a letter from her friend, thanking her for helping her avoid a grave decision. It appeared that Mrs Munsiff's friend had decided to end it all when the postman came. She had decided to read her mail for the last when she was delighted by a letter from her old friend. This helped her avoid an unsuitable decision.

Marenghez Munsiff

Marenghez also mentioned that when we visit the Shrines in Haifa we should be in our best behavior. While on pilgrimage, she would change saris every day in order to meet the Shrines in something new that she liked, especially if she were to meet the Guardian, who lived in her time. However, she did not wish for too much insistence on respect the part of others for her having met the Guardian, such that such respect becomes unseemly. She also repeated that we remember that there is no kissing of others' hands in the Faith, as a religious action.

AFTER THE INTERNATIONAL BAHA'I CONVENTION OF 1978

Edward Ntsangani near his home at Kwazakhele, Port Elizabeth.

 In 1978 I attended the International Baha'i Convention in Haifa, Israel as a delegate for the election of the Universal House of Justice. On my return, I found the Baha'is and several other people enthusiastic about the Faith. Edward was one of such people and at the time he was a member f the Local Spiritual Assembly of Kwazakhele. Port Elizabeth. We had met at junior high school and later worked in the same department at employment for over thirteen years.

A QUESTION POSED

This question is posed by Edward and many other Baha'is. This question has mainly been answered by now but in the olden days it was an obstacle to teaching the Faith. This includes and involves how to view a Baha'i community of a composition of many levels of people, especially in Africa. Many Africans accepted the change offered by the Faith but it came at what was perceived to be leaving customs and olden ways. As a result many people would insist on being accepted as they were and not as strangers to themselves. Thozi is friends with Ronald Fudu and myself but does not wish to be extensively altered from what is accepted by other Africans.

With the translation of the Writings and laws of the Faith into African languages, this attitude has by far vanished. This is evidenced by the fact that the Baha'i Faith has been accepted by government authorities to the extent of being granted times of service on the Radio System. The songs and activities of Baha'is are not any farther from African behavior than other activities of communities in the country. The Baha'i Faith is being recognized as a distinct religion of a certain definite character and a Baha'i is the every day person met everywhere except that the Baha'i has to know what hurts the Faith and what does not..

This does not mean that all the teachings and laws of the Faith are acceptable to everyone but they are known even if not believable by many. There is always the doubt that uniting the world could occur. The Baha'is are not daunted but work patiently and quietly in teaching their Faith to all. Their peaceful ways are appreciated. Edward still associates with Baha'is but is isolated in Kwazakhele, far from activities. With time, he will join in.

There is an attitude which binds Africans together. It is the result of a common belief in customs and Ancestors. All that they are involved in outwardly is unimportant when customs are approached. The defining position in such a unity, is not one's station in life today, nor is it one's education. It is how much one knows and respects the custom. Religion is closely associated with customs as it points to that which is invisible to the eye. In that kind of involvement one is also defined by how much the religion is understood and again not by any material station. To remain in the bond one has to be loyal to the bond because, in commonality, one finds that one needs others to perform certain rights and customs within the group.

Such an attitude avoids the separation into the educated and uneducated, as all are seen as one by both the religion and common African beliefs. If then one wants to find those who will want to have a deeper meaning of the Baha'i Faith, one is at a loss in how to take the educated aside and deepen them. This would seem to separate a group as being better than the rest and that is not accepted. Africans then can only be approached the African way in order not to cause disruptions. Perhaps this is why such violence was exhibited against those who chose to support a union that was outside the main unity. Safe ground is to use African attitudes within the context of African life and relate that to African attitudes, or customs if one likes. Otherwise teaching the Western way does not work. Choosing a middle culture like the Baha'i

Faith one has to build on what the other cultures have and incorporate such behaviors in the new ways. The success of a barbecue owes itself to that, as it is a condition that is related both to African ways and sacrifice for a cause. Thozi and many others attach more importance to refusal to being foreigners to themselves. That being understood, we continue with the story.

THE WEDDING OF GRACE AND RONALD FUDU

When I went to Haifa I was living in this house which soon became a place where many Baha'i meetings were held until I moved out leaving Ronald Fudu to occupy the house as a newly wed.

The house in which the Assembly of Zwide met and where Ronald Grace Fudu were married

Ronald and Grace Fudu's Baha'i marriage was performed here and a social, celebrating the wedding was also held the next day in the same house.

Ronald and Grace Fudu at the social.

A group at the wedding

TRANSLATIONS

From 1968 several booklets had been translated, and this made it far easier to communicate the meaning of the Baha'i Faith, as the condition had been when many Writings were translated from the original text into English by the Guardian. Apart from a prayer book and institutes of Baha'i laws and principles, none of the major works of the Faith had been available in African languages.

On my street was Millicent Dzingwe's house. As a school teacher Millicent had a typewriter. I took advantage of this. I asked her if I could look after her house while she went to the Transkei on vacation that December and she consented to the plan. I was not used to a typewriter, but alone in her house I could make all the mistakes I was going to make on the typewriter without interruption. This started me on translations and more importantly, on Baha'i activities. Later, Millicent was to allow us to hold meetings in a classroom in her school. Nomvula and Millicent were good friends and also were related. Both were very encouraging as I took my first steps in this task. (Nomvula went so far as to assist me in helping me and my wife when I married a second time). A series of booklets and letters were translated at this time until a "corona" typewriter was purchased by the National Assembly while I was travelling. This is merely a digression, the main story being the translation of one of the major works of Baha'u'llah, the *Kitab-i-Iqan* or The Book of Certitude.

THE TRANSLATION OF THE BOOK OF CERTITUDE

This story is mentioned at this point because it was at this time that the translation took a very serious turn, as the National Assembly enquired about the Book.

Regardless of that, the letter requesting the translation of the Book of Certitude was received in 1972 and translation began almost immediately. The Book of Certitude was initially called the *Risaliy-i-Khal* (Epistle to the Uncle) before being designated by Baha'u'llah as the *Kitab-i-Iqan*(The Book of Certitude). It was written as an answer to questions of the uncle of the Báb, in two nights and two days(Taherzadeh, p. 158).

First the text had to be written in longhand and then the typing would begin. In my limited Xhosa which is gleaned from school and church the effort of writing down what I thought was every word took almost a year. After this the translation was abandoned. I am no typist and the fastest I can go with two fingers is twenty five words per minute.

Two years into the translation I was elected to the National Spiritual Assembly of South Africa..

During one meeting the issue of the translations was raised .Doctor Michael Walker who was on the National Literature Committee, enquired on progress on the translation. When he was informed of my dilemma, he suggested helping with sending books on typing lessons, as well as some Xhosa dictionaries. He insisted that we validate every word with words used in the *Bible*. We then used the *King James Version* of the Bible as he pointed out that this had been used in translating quotes from that Book. Validation and authentication proved hard but rewarding. Many words which are no longer used in common, spoken Xhosa language were found in the Bible and used as such. I am certain that my father who was an herbalist would have had meanings for myrtles and jasmines but I had none, so I coined words. There are no separate words for "spirit" and "soul" in Xhosa and this was a difficulty; neither were names I knew for "Constantinople" or "Adrianople". Many words had to be written as pronounced phonetically.

Mike took on the task of looking for a publisher in Cape Town. Having found one, there followed for me reading and editing galley-proofs at night. Each set of proofs had to be dispatched by morning. One of the Baha'i pioneers offered to pay for publishing the Book if we met a deadline of having it done by Ridvan of 1979. In order to catch-up with the typing, I had had to employ three typists in the Transkei, while I was attempting to pioneer there.

The translation was completed by 1979 and the National Assembly presented me with a signed copy. Doctor Michael Walker got the pleasure of having accomplished this effort and moved on to the next task.

REFLECTIONS AFTER TRANSLATING THE BOOK OF CERTITUDE

After reading the Kitab-i-Iqan for the first time entirely, in 1970, an effort which took me the better part of a sleepless night to complete, I was left with a question which took me years to answer. The question was about understanding a statement I found in that Book. In fact, there were two statements about the same issue , but the result were words of exclamation that ran :" Athim in the Book of God; mighty among the common herd; Karim in name!"(Kitab-i-Iqan, p. 190)

Baha'u'llah tells a story about Haji Mirza Karim Khan-i-Kirmani, a Doctor of Islamic Law and a writer. Karim Khan had claimed to be the Promised One at some stage and later contented himself with opposing the Baha'i Faith. Karim Khan had a great following and had written a number of books. Baha'u'llah was requested by some believers to look at some of these books and He refused. However, He decided to look through one book which had the title :"Guidance for the Ignorant" In the book Karim Khan calls himself the "Athim Servant". This latter is a feigned humility. In the Qur'an Muhammad says :" The Athim(sinner) shall eat of the Zaqqum(an evil tree in the Next World)" Later in the text Muhammd wrote" Taste thou of this for thou art Karim(honorable)". (Kitab-i-Iqan, p. 190)

Once I met a Persian man who understood both Farsi and Arabic, Sadri Farabi, and asked him the same question that I had asked many people over the years. Sadri felt that he could only try to explain if he read the Arabic text in the original form, as he understood very little English.

The next time I met Sadri, he gave me the text in these words": Karimun fel ism, Athimun fil Kitab, azizun baynul an am!"

After thinking this over and adding to it that Sadri said the man used to write many negative articles about the Baha'i Faith in newspapers, and realizing that the man had influence, I had the feeling that Muhammad had written about Karim some thousand years before he came the oppose of the Baha'i Faith.

I further inquired about the man, Karim , and what he was. I found that he was described as a person who had seven qualities all beginning with the letter "K" in Arabic: He was obese; he was short; he had no beard, he was bald; he was from Kirman, he was an nonbeliever(infidel) ; and he was one-eyed. In some way, these disqualified him from being the Promised One, for the text of Traditions was clear that the Promised one would have no defects in his body. The other two men who claimed this title were also too tall; one eyed and obese.

This statement seemed to point at us that we flock to that which is popular and discard the truth, even though we have been warned to look out for such. This is how my thinking runs about this part of the text, and I may even be wrong.

TRANSLATING INTO AFRIKAANS

The Kitab-i-Iqan was made available in Afrikaans through the efforts of Gottfried Winckler, assisted by Michael Walker. The National Assembly was consulted on appropriate words to use, to a certain point, in both languages, Xhosa and Afrikaans..

(L-R) Gottfried Winckler with Bishop Brown and Bahiyyih Winckler

RENEWED ACTIVITY IN NEW BRIGHTON

Elijah Mancayi

In 1979 I moved back to New Brighton. There were a number of active Baha'is at this time. They included Elijah Mancayi whom I knew from childhood, Christopher Buyambo, with whom I was a server in the Anglican Church and Reginald Vimbi, whose father I had worked with at the Livingstone Hospital in the mid-fifties..

DAWN PRAYERS

Each morning at dawn, I would meet with first Elijah at his home and then proceed to Reginald's before taking the bus to work. This worked out as an activity for a while.

I visited Christopher who was an artist many times, as he had been elected to the Local Spiritual Assembly of New Brighton. We arranged many meetings some of which were not too successful even though arranging them was an activity in itself. Christopher passed on while I was in Swaziland but his daughters were very welcoming when I came on visits.

Nomahlubi Buyambo one of Christopher's daughters who is now a school teacher

AFTER THE DEPARTURE OF THE BEERS

A STORY OF SURVIVAL

Sue Greer

Bonnie Moore

 In 1979 I made an attempt at pioneering in the Transkei. Two people gave a hand in that effort; Sue Greer and Bonnie Moore. Both of them encouraged me to seek ways of finding work and pioneering. I needed to settle as a citizen in the country in order to find work. Transkei had its homeland independence. I applied for a passport and was surprised at the fees I had to pay. I was more or less penniless after my stay for so long away from work and home. Bonnie supplied the money for the passport and I was able to be granted one based on also my friendship with the Ndungane family who were employed by the government and had no lack of relatives in the proper places.

When I had the passport, I had to find work and find it soon. Sue Greer offered to take me around to companies where I could find employment. Every time we failed in one company, Sue would amusingly say:"Stick around , baby, I'm going to make you famous!", and we would proceed to the next company. I soon found work with the Xhosa Development Corporation a

Transkeian organization which had connections with many companies in the country. I was to manage a gasoline delivery service by staying in touch with delivery trucks. However, I was to leave an address where I could be contacted. Having done that, I returned home to Port Elizabeth.

Things went very wrong when the corporation called me at work, and my manager denied that there was such a person in his employ. That robbed me of all chances of credibility and the opportunity was also gone. It did not matter what I said later, my manger was believed entirely. So I stayed at my original employment and found out my job had already been advertized. It took help from the National Assembly to get the authorities to accept me under very stringent conditions.

TEACHING PLAN

After the Beers left there were many plans for the region. One of them was the *"each one teach one plan"*

In 1981, the National Teaching Committee had a teaching plan termed "Each one teach one". It was at this time that Laurie Konstant arrived in Port Elizabeth accompanied by two youths from the Cape Town community: Aaron and Rida. The purpose was to increase teaching activities in the Colored area. The three had a song that encouraged teaching, and it had the words:

> Each one teach one
> Travel through the land.
> Together, individually
> Reach the heart of man.

> Each one teach one
> Watch our numbers grow.
> If each would teach
> We we'd have one world for Baha'u'llah.

I have never been able to forget that song.

Laurie is Canadian in origin and both Aaron and Rida are Malay. Therefore, we had to meet in the Colored area. We found a place at the *Alabama Hotel* where they reserved *the Blue Room* for our use. Each morning we met there and said prayers and then Aaron , Rida and I would proceed out to teach. We had joyous times doing door-to-door teaching in Gelvandale Township and other townships. After a week, the three had to leave. It was with a sad heart that we parted, but we retained happy memories and had learned new strategies in teaching.

THE COMING OF
EGHBAL AND SARAH MA'ANI

EGHBAL AND SARAH ARRIVE

Eghbal must have become interested in pioneering in Port Eliza-
beth when once asked by the National Assembly to deliver a type-
writer to me while he was on a trip which passed through my town.

For some years the African friends had carried on their tasks until around
1981 when Eghbal and Sarah Ma'ani, who had just got married , moved into
town. First these two pioneers settled in the area of Walmer, farther than the
center of the city, and later moved closer to the city center. Their home was
easily accessible on foot from the city. These were harder days and required
Baha'is who understood the bravery of self-sacrifice. They were as diverse in
family composition as Rosemary and Emeric Sala who had first settled in Summerstrand on the beachfront had been. Eghbal was Persian in origin when
Sarah was American. This age and combination of cultures thrilled the Baha'is
because both pioneers from the States and Persia were represented in them.
Eghbal had been educated in the United Kingdom and become a civil engineer there. Sarah had come as a very young, brave girl from the Sates to pioneer in South Africa on her own. Her first task on arrival was to assist the
National Secretary in his work. The two, Ehbal and Sarah had met when appointed by the National Assembly to the National Youth Committee.

The bravery they showed in entering the townships at night and during
weekends was astounding. This activity was done in such a way that to an on-
looker it was casual yet they both knew the tests which Africans were going
through at that time and the real dangers involved. Yet they showed no fear
but rather concentrated on the task at hand, mainly the teaching of their Faith,
and being part and parcel of activities in the townships and the greater Cape
Midlands.

Nomkhita Funani, taught by Shelley Cook, was present when Eghbal gave a talk on Early Baha'i History one night at my home. At this time the riots were on.

NOMKHITA AND SHELLEY COOK

Nomkhitha had been a chief prefect at Buntingville Boarding School in Umtata where Shelley Cook taught. She had been taught the Faith at this school by Shelley, before she moved to live in New Brighton on completing high school education. Her name had been included on the list of Baha'is residing in Port Elizabeth. Sarah, Eghbal, Nomabhadi, my wife, and I found her at her home , when we searched for Baha'is in the township, at the suggestion of the Ma'anis'. I had lived for nearly six years away from New Brighton, and did not know who had left or arrived. .Nomkhitha had two little sisters and they all had problems of residence. At the suggestion of Nomabhadi and Nomkhitha's mother, the three girls came to reside with my family, as I had a larger house, at the time, which I was buying from the Township Authorities.

In order to help the girls, we decided to have a deepening class at my home, where Sarah and Eghbal would deliver lessons in the evenings until the girls' mother found room for them elsewhere. This event occurred sometime in 1983.

THE RESPECTED GUEST IN MDANTSANE

Hand of the Cause
William Sears
(From Personal
collection of pictures)

The son of the Hand of the Cause William Sears, Michael Sears , who was at this time the chairman of the National Assembly was also known as a notable speaker, as witnessed at closing of National Conventions and at deepening classes around Johannesburg. The Hand of the Cause had often visited his family in Johannesburg and given talks to groups in that area. However, since Mdantsnae was a relatively new Baha'i locality, he had not as yet given talks there or in that vicinity. As the news spread that he was to come , so did the excitement increase. He was known to be in the Transkei *en route* to the Eastern Cape, while engaged in writing another book of the title *All Flags Flying*.

There was held at that time a summer school at Mdantsane , and the Hand of the Cause William Sears was expected to arrive at any moment. The summer school was held in a school hall. The end of the summer school was delayed to accommodate the arrival of our visitor. However, the summer school had to give up and was closing. All were disappointed and began to pack up. It was at that moment that Hand of the Cause William Sears arrived. Everybody returned to their seats hastily, in front of the tent which had been erected around a main stand. As Hand of the Cause William Sears prepared to talk the Audio Visual Officer , Sirus Mahmoudi, quickly set up video cameras to record the occasion.

The subject was *Progressive Revelation*. In a brief but effective way, the Hand of the Cause demonstrated this important Baha'i theme so that all gained some insights. All that while, he had his audience rolling with laughter while seriously making his point. At the end of his talk he remarked that he had everybody laughing because he did not wish to tire his audience as they had been talking of spiritual matters all week He jokingly called the condition we might suffer "spiritual combatits". That had everybody laughing even more. This visit is also dealt with in *This Side Up* (Mazibuko, 2010)

THE BACKGROUND TO THE TALK

As this was the first time that the Hand of the Cause spoke at a summer school in Mdantsane, something should be said about how this came about. Prior to the talk, the Hand of the Cause William Sears was visiting relatives by the name of the del Moro who were residing in the Transkei at the time. During this time also, Mr Sears was writing a book called *All Flags Flying*. On the decision to go to Mdantsane and see the Baha'i friends, he had to complete a dictation of 600 pages of the book to Margaret Piggott who was engaged in typing and retyping the book to ready it for publishing. This task of preparing the manuscript had to be completed before the talk. One would then imagine that he was very tired by the time he travelled to Mdantsane, hence the lateness of arrival. He explained al this himself as an apology for his arriving at that hour. His first statement was that he had not had time to prepare a talk but was ready with r inspiration to give a talk.

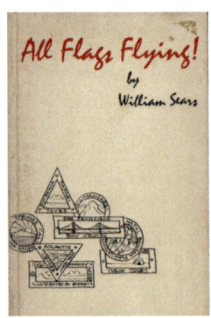

A picture of the cover of book the Hand of the Cause William Sears, was writing in 1982.

Regardless of the tiredness, Mr Sears was still a Baha'i teacher answering current questions that were related to the area he was in. He chose as his subject "Progressive Revelation" and related it to the possibility of adaptation to the situation of travelling teacher in that area and the available resources. He had carried a copy of the Bible from which he made quotes of the prophecies fulfilled by the coming of Baha'u'llah. Translating for him was an experience, because he felt it when I made an explanation instead of a direct translation and followed the translation with humor and seriousness. Perhaps his past stay in Africa had made him aware of the different African languages spoken there. He deliberately mentioned the words "make it up, if you do not remember what I said", knowing very well that I could not do that. The *Kitab-i-Iqan* had just been translated , and in this way a test was applied to see just how serious translations were being done. I believed from his remarks that the translator passed any test in that quarter. When he mentioned relatives in Milwaukee, WI, he quipped that someday the translator would translate for him there, a statement which had all, including the translator laughing hard. His attitude of being so humorous relaxed the atmosphere enough for the translator to quickly reflect on his last statements, between the laughter of the house, before translating. This was a great help. It also meant that the translator had to concentrate, a feat which was somewhat hard under the lighting of the video equipment to which he was not accustomed. Reflecting on the strength of the Hand of the Cause, particularly at his age, I find he was quite amazing because the talk was arranged on the spur of the moment and yet it was so successful. The summer school was terminated on a high note of success.

A letter from the Hand of the Cause.

Some years later when I reached the United States, I wrote to the Hand of the Cause William Sears and received a note from him and his wife, Marguerite Sears:

" June 1, 1991
Allah'u'abha!

Dear Robert,

Thank you so much for writing such a lovely letter. I am always gladdened to hear from Friends who have grown in their Faith and love for Baha'u'llah. Thank you for reminding me of that telephone call and I am pleased that the book has found a home with you and your family. Your remembrance was most kind and deeply appreciated.

Warmest Baha'i greetings,

William Sears.

Hand of the Cause of God.

Dear Robert, Allah'u'Abha!

It was good to hear from you. Mike was here in part of March & April for Bill's 80th birthday…They had not been together in 18 yrs.

The book, if it's "Thief" Dizzy sent to Bill saying it was his declaration of his faith in Baha'u'llah.

All good wishes,
Marguerite."

SOME IMPORTANT EVENTS EXPERIENCED WITH EGHBAL AND SARAH

The longer part of the story of this family is told in the book *This Side Up* (Mazibuko , 2010)

Sarah and Eghbal Ma'ani (extreme left of picture with Sarah carrying a childe) at Convention in Umgababa, near Durban with African bah'is from Port Elizabeth

Ridvan John Ma'ani eldest son of the Ma'anis

A MEETING AT THE MA'ANIS'

In 1985 Sarah's parents who worked at the World Center came on a visit, the friends gathered at the Ma'anis' to see them.

Baha'is at he home of the Ma'anis'

(Picture taken after moving from Port Elizabeth. Faran was a baby in 1987) Sarah Ma'ani with the youngest son, Far'an.

BOOK SALES OFFICER VISITS PORT ELIZABETH

The Book Sales store had a new manager and he was interested in having more Baha'is buy books. This would prove a protection by making them knowledgeable of the history of the Faith and acquaint them with many important events. It would then be harder for anyone to try to get them off the path of faith. The Officer that year was Dr Robert Clarkson, a lecturer at the University of the Witwatersrand, by profession. In order to achieve his goal, he travelled through the country with a load of books.

In Port Elizabeth, he set up a modest exhibition of what was available and had arranged for local Baha'is to visit. The results of this effort can best be described by the officer involved because at that time, very few Africans had the wish to assemble in the white area, indeed , it was advisable not to, but instead to find time in the day to go as individuals to see hat to buy, and that was the option I chose.

A NATIONAL MEETING IN
NEW BRIGHTON IN MIDDLE EIGHTIES

Meetings amongst the Baha'is of New Brighton were held in schools or hotels because it was easier to negotiate with a sympathetic private sector than to obtain a permit from the government for a public meeting. It was, therefore an unusual step taken by the National Administration that a national meeting be planned to be held in New Brighton. However, circumstances had greatly changed. It was now possible to hold public meetings in the Transkei and the Ciskei and the Ciskei had attained a form of independence. This was so serious that entrance into the Ciskei was by travel document.

Having such a meeting within the township necessitated drastic arrangements. A written permit had to come from the offices of the Township Manager, both for holding a meeting in the Centenary Hall, and for all black and white Baha'is who would enter the township during that conference.

Even though this event occurred during a riotous period in New Brighton, these tasks were performed easily and the conference was held. The important thing was to watch for all Baha'is entering the township and direct them to the hall in order to avoid anyone found wandering in the streets looking for the hall.

The Baha'i Faith in South Africa had come out of obscurity and had become known even more than before. We avoided looking like tourists with cameras around shoulders, therefore very few Africans thought of taking any pictures. Those available would have been taken by the Audio-Visual Office who by now has passed on to the Next World. The joy of seeing our friends from so far afield was enough to make their existence a reality and not a distant dream we experienced. This took place near 1983 or 1984, however, time and date could be established by the National Teaching Committees, as this was partly the plan of that committee.

THE TWO DEATHS

Phillip Ntsetha with Ronald Fudu at a Unit Convention held in a school room at Charles Duna Primary School.

PHILLIP NTSETHA

Phillip in the picture with Ronald declared on my return from Haifa in 1978, but soon took part in political activity. He was *necklaced* after frantically calling me by telephone from hiding in the middle of the night. He is well remembered with sorrow that he could not receive the political help and physical aid he needed.

Philip called at about ten p.m. and asked for help. He never explained the kind of help he needed. On asking where he was he replied that his parents knew where he was, and that one could go to them to get directions. As the writer was living alone at the time and serving on the Baha'i National Assembly, he thought it a wise move to talk to the Secretary of the National Assembly before taking any steps. He knew that Phillip had joined a political organization and he had cautioned him about Baha'i Law that prohibits such involvement.. At the time, he had promised to withdraw from politics. The Secretary, a veteran of WW II replied that if the writer went in search of the man then he would be implicated and perceived to know more than he did and even involve other Baha'is in the area or region. His advice was that the man should come to the writer for the writer to advise him.

Phillip never called again. In a few days the newspapers reported his atrocious death. On hearing the sad news, the writer approached a neighbor to inquire about why the man needed help. It transpired that Phillip had been wrongly accused of a crime committed by someone else who was involved in political action. He had been arrested and released only to be accused of being an informer. He then went in hiding and unfortunately been found..

THAMSANQA TSHIKILA

The second man to suffer death in this fashion was Thamsanqa Tshikila. He had come to ask the writer to find work for him since his company had reduced staff due to the disinvestment decision, and he had been affected in the reduction of staff. The writer was approached by his younger brother who worked as a foreman to find employment for Thamie in his company. The writer was not a member of the Trade Union but he approached the Shop Stewards and asked for work on behalf of his Baha'i friend. There was promise of work but nothing definite. So Thamsanqa had to wait. Before becoming a Baha'i Thamie had dabbled in crime but he had decided to lead a straight life.

For some weeks the writer did not see Thamsanqa. One day the Shop Steward asked him to present himself at the Main Gate as there was a vacancy. After work, the writer went in search of Thamie and found his girlfriend who promised that he would take the job since she was then pregnant and they wished to marry.

The next morning, Thamie turned up masked in a heavy coat to the ears, and asked for the job but he arrived very late. When the authorities were approached Thamie was told that he had arrived too late to take the job and it had been given to someone else. He then went home.

That weekend Thamie was shot and *neckaced*. I was told that he had been in hiding before after an accusation of possession, and had been released. For reasons I do not know, he was also accused of being an informer as he knew and had contacted a wanted supplier on behalf of someone else. Since all this is hearsay I shall not dwell on it but I am certain Thamie wanted to live a straight life and had chosen the Baha'i Faith as his religion I can only say that my little brother who was his close friend vouches for him and holds him innocent. I had asked him to go to work. It pains me to know that I had asked him to come out of hiding, but I did not know and still do not know all the facts of his case. There was a strike when we were not to go to employment and Thamie had spent the day at my home listening to music with me.

Both these cases are a source of sadness to me because in both cases there was an appeal I failed to bring to a successful conclusion.

AN ATTEMPT AT TEACHING

After the pilgrimage and before leaving South Africa in 1985 several attempts to teach within the township were made by myself and two youths from New Brighton. However, these attempts failed due to the atmosphere prevailing at the time.

Some youth from New Brighton. Some went teaching with me.

In an effort to still the tumult of the country, the government had imported *vigilantes* to patrol the townships and restore order. *Vigilantes* were known to be *Zulu*-speaking. If they found anybody loitering in the late hours, they could beat that person with sticks even to death. This part is told because it has a bearing on the story.

One adult, my self, and two young men went out to teach the Baha'i Faith in Kwazakhele. The year was 1985 and that day there was a quiet in the rioting.

We got to Kwazakhele in the early afternoon, and randomly chose a house. In accordance with African manners the tree sat down and proceeded to introduce themselves and the news of the Baha'i Faith. The adult man noticed that, in one corner of the house was a man who appeared to be drunk, but in the small kitchen, the lady of the home seemed to be listening. It so happened that the adult Baha'i's name was *Zulu*. As soon as this was announced, the man in the corner, who had appeared to be asleep, came suddenly alive and asked for the *Zulu* last name to be repeated.

When the drunken man was sure this was what he had heard, he angrily voiced the grievance that the *Vigilantes* were not giving anyone any rest or peace and he could hardly visit at night without fearing them. Now a man with a *Zulu* last name was in his house: why not wreak vengeance and sacrifice him? He then menacingly approached the three Baha'is with fingers outspread in a gripping stance.

The lady in the kitchen, fearing disaster for the three, grabbed the drunken man, threw to the floor, and yelled that the three should hurry out of the house.

In the street, the three Baha'is were undaunted and wanted to try again. They chose a second house and found an older lady to talk to. They introduced the Baha'i Faith as a religion of God. Suddenly there came into the room a young man. Obviously he was unfriendly towards the three Baha'is. He pointed out that his family had a church in which they worshiped; that at that time they were not worshiping because they had a battle to fight; and that when all the fighting was done, then they could think of worship. He demanded that the three should leave before there was serious trouble.

The three Baha'is left and considered it a bad day for teaching, and so they returned d home to New Brighton.

SARAH AND EGHBAL IN THE CAPE MIDLANDS

Both of the children of the Ma'anis' , Ridvan John and Faran, were born in Port Elizabeth before the Ma'anis moved out. Ridvan John was named after both his grand-fathers ,Nabil Ma'ani and John Conklin, while Faran was named such that if we remembered Paran in the *Bible* we would remember his name. Eghbal passed on at the early age of forty eight.

In the time Eghbal and Sarah were there the Faith spread to Cradock and participation in the Colored area was enhanced. Cradock had Baha'is who served on National Committee and one, Vuyelwa Mbotya, actually travelled to New York to participate in the Baha'i World Congress held there in 1992, a year which marked the Commemoration hundredth year after the Ascension of Baha'u'llah.

TEACHING IN THE EASTERN CAPE

Teaching in the Eastern Cape

 The conferences, summer schools and other deepening meetings held in schools and public places in the Mdatsane area were attended by Baha'is from many levels of society. No one was rejected and cultural dress was adequately modified by Africans to blend with the rest of society found at meetings. However, for the most part, original unassuming cultural dress was used. The acceptability of the African language and culture made many Africans feel free to express themselves at meetings and to attend without any fears of embarrassment. The Baha'i World Center had set the standard of accepting any garb from any land at the International Convention and this example was followed with joy.

The teaching of the equality of men and women convinced more women to adhere to the Baha'i Faith as their religion. Many women were influential in the Faith and some functioned as travelling teachers both in the cities and the rural areas.

The Friends had learned that the criteria for belief were not the way one dressed; not the music one preferred,; not the language one spoke, not even the amount of intelligence they possessed , but the ability to believe in the Faith and the extent each internalized the teachings of that Faith. Many a time has an intelligent person been debarred from belief in a new Manifestation from God!

Summer schools were where Baha'is practiced living a Baha'i life, whereas, Conventions were meetings where Baha'is demonstrated the working of their administration and elected their Administrative Bodies. Though only delegates could speak at Conventions, the attendance by non-delegates was generally good. The Baha'is from Mdantsane were noticeable at National Conferences and Conventions at about the seventies.

A school hall where a Baha'i summer school was held at Mdantsnae.

(Esther Nkonzo is in the extreme right with believers from the Eastern Cape villages. On her left is Reinette Ndubaza from Ngqumeya) Esther and Reinette were travelling teachers .

(Picture by author)

Another meeting in a school room, attended by all groups

Baha'is around Rose Gates' car in the rural areas(in front row, LR, Esther Nkonzo, Beauty Kato, Maria Manentsa, with two unidentified men.)

(Picture by Rose Gates)

A group at the National Convention at Umgababa near Durban

Some of the styles of dresses worn by some Baha'is

A BAHA'I LOCAL ASSEMBLY IN MDANTSANE

Mdantsane formed a functioning Assembly and had an Area Teaching Committee appointed before the administration began to grow in Port Elizabeth. For a while I served on that Area Teaching Committee. All this occurred in the very short time that Rose Gates settled in East London. The Local Spiritual Assembly of Mdantsane was able to handle even marriages, including that of Robert Mazibuko and Faith Kato.

SOME BAHA'IS FROM THE CISKEI

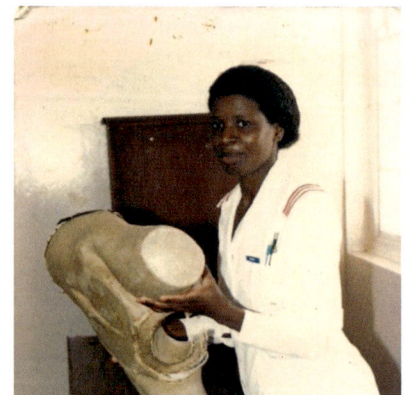

Vumeka Rungqu who was a recently declared Baha'i when I visited in 1987

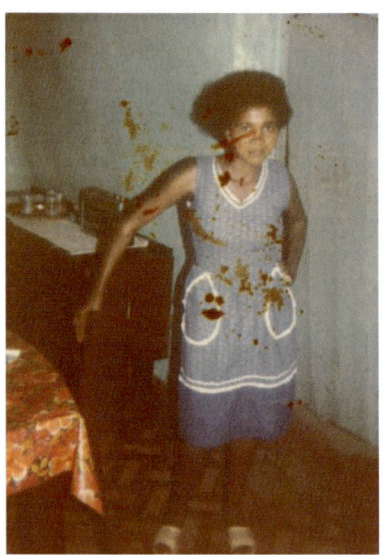

Zameka Ngalwana a children's class teacher at Ngqumeya Baha'i Center

Ngqumeya , a village in the Eastern Cape had a beautiful Baha'i Center where meetings were held. Near this Center was a room used for children's classes. Zameka Ngalwana was the main teacher at this Center when I travelled there under the Ciskeian National Assembly in 1987. The two teachers with whom I travelled went out to teach with me in Keiskammahoek and Zwelitsha. I was also accompanied in Zwelitsha by Esther Nkonzo of Mdantsane and Riaz Razavi of Kingwilliamstown. .

A TEACHER FROM NEW YORK

It was a cold winter—cold in terms of South Africa—when I was asked to travel-teach in Ciskei. I had just arrived in the country from Swaziland and residing in Soweto, part of the time. I was not quite prepared for the hospitality the friends in Mdantsane had in store for me. Knowing that I would be low in personal funds after my pioneering in Swaziland, the friends had gone to a lot of trouble in even buying new clothing for me to wear and arranging a place to stay. I felt at home. I touch upon these details because I met a travelling teacher who accepted any kind of environment offered.

I had met with Riaz Razavi and Esther Nkonzo and had taught in Zwelitsha, Kingwilliamston with them. Now I was with the Scotts' family in Alice. I was told that there was a visitor from New York in the house. Her name was Noushin('Noushin', I learned, means a sweet dream one has before waking up). It took time to realize that Noushin was a university teacher but that did not seem to be too important to her at that time. She wanted to see African Baha'is and meet them where they lived.

After a pilgrimage she had decided to plunge into a visit first to Kenya and now was in the Ciskei. Ciskei had just formed a National Assembly. The greater part of the community near Alice lived in *roundavels* built in villages outside of towns. We determined to visit some of the villages, and Noushin asked if she could spend the week in the village. I was astounded! How was she going to do this? She had asked for no special food or amenities but was sure she wanted to spend a week in the village.

One morning we took her with us to visit a village. She was welcomed and accommodated in a *roundavel* by the African friends. We had to leave her there at her insistence.

On returning, after a week, we found her still smiling and dressed in African style with a scarf on her head! The African friends were excited and thrilled to be with her. I promised that when I got to the United States I would call her at her work, and I did! Her short tale about herself proved very true and the lesson she taught was valuable.

THE TRAVELLING TEACHERS

The growth of the Faith spread into the wider area of the Cape Midlands with Local Assemblies in Grahamstown, Mossel Bay Uitenhage and Cradock.

Some teachers from the Eastern Cape helped, not only with encouragement but with visits to the areas where they had relatives in the Cape Midlands and Eastern Cape.. For example Mthembu and Ivy Gcume helped introduce the Faith to Somerset East and Cradock.

In the Eastern Cape, Esther Nkonzo and Joyce Dwashu travelled into many villages and established so many communities that by 1985 there was a Baha'i Center in Ngquneya established with the assistance of Reinette Ndubaza and Cynthia Ngodwane who resided in those areas.

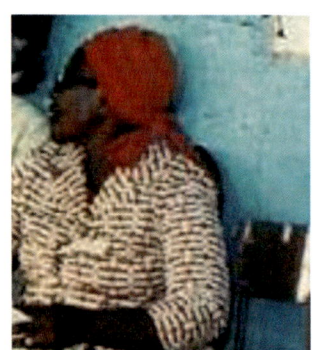

Joyce Dwashu   *Esther Nkonzo*

By 1985 a national Community was established in the homeland of Ciskei, this areas included Zwelitsha, Mdantsane , Ginsburg, Keiskammahoek,

St Matthews, Ngqumeya, Middledrift, Burnshill , Fort Cox, Peddie, Alice and several other towns and villages where Baha'is had contacts. This whole home-land was incorporated into South Africa when that country had a democratic government.

The Baha'i Faith was spread throughout the Eastern Cape through a few dedicate women, most of whom were later elected to the National Assembly of the Ciskei in 1985. It is interesting to note that the grave of one of these women is located next to that of the "three Martyrs of Mdantsane".

Eight of the members of the National Assembly of the Ciskei elected in 1985 (picture taken in 1987)

The grave of Esther Nkonzo , a travelling-teacher, which is located next to that of Shamam, Hushmund and Riaz.

113

The first teacher in the Eastern Cape, Rose Gates
(taken with R. Mazibuko on, Mt Carmel, Haifa in 1978)

A STAY IN SWAZILAND

 In September of 1985, I moved to Swaziland where I rented a house near Manzini. I had meant to live in Swaziland and marry there, but because my spouse was unable to settle there I had to leave for the United States from where.

Because I meant to live in Swaziland , I sold all I had and furnished the house with everything I felt was necessary for one to live there. I had brought some furniture from South Africa and had it freighted to Swaziland and bought even more items while residing in Swaziland. There was a store near my employment where I could buy at arranged prices because the company had business dealing with my employers. All this was done in preparation for the arrival of my bride to be. When she came in April of 1986, I proudly showed her the home I had intended for us. The area I had settled in , with the help of Debbie Dadgar and Rachmah Michelle Wolf, was Zakhele in Manzini.

A view of the neighborhood through a window.

*Gretchen on arrival in Swazi-
land(1986).*

*Gretchen in the house in Zakhele
Manzini(1986).*

Near Matsapa airport, Manzini, where Gretchen arrived

It was unfortunate that at this time I had lost my job. I had then applied to the National Assembly of Swaziland to do travel teaching in Swaziland and been accepted. Before and after Gretchen's visit, I pursued my travel-teaching activities in Swaziland, spending much time on the road. I had occasion to visit Maputo where I had been assigned to work. I had known Maputo only through the LM Radio station in the days it was called Lorenzo Marques. It struck me as a very silent place, except for the many quaint motor cars I saw on the streets. Most people were subdued. I did not stay long, just about a night and a day. In that short time, I was taught a lot about the business I was employed in by the company in Swaziland which had several branches one of which was in Maputo..

A friend who showed me around his area in Swaziland while I was travel-teaching.

A children's class I held at the Baha'i Center in Havelock Mining compound , Swaziland

In Maputo, Mozambique near where I resided on a visit

AN UNEXPECTED EVENT

A few months after my arrival in Swaziland it was announced that a visitor from Haifa, Israel was coming to Swaziland. We were to assemble at Massoud and Mujgand Derrakhshani's house to welcome the visitor and have a session with him. Our visitor was Hasan Sabri who served at the Baha'i World Center.

On the day of the appointment we had a full house and listened to a short talk by Hasan Sabri. He talked about the Baha'i Faith and people; that the Faith was composed of people and its activities executed by such people. Therefore it mattered that the friends take their work very seriously. I perceived him as saying:"Let your light so shine before men , that they may see your works and glorify your Father Who is in heaven" (*Holy Bible: Matthew 5:16*) or in the words of Baha'u'llah:"Let deeds not words be your adorning!"(*The Hidden Words: Persian # 5*)

After the talk Hasan Sabri went around the room shaking hands and hugging everyone. It was inspiring to find him there because we were certain this was not a random or accidental visit. We all felt honored. I had heard many times of Hasan Sabri and Isonbel Sabri(Associated with the International Goals Committee) through the Baha'i newsletters and had met Hasan once only in Haifa in 1985, but this was the first time I heard give a talk...

*Hasan Sabri, shaking hands
with Azam Mossoun
(Namati) during visit in
Swaziland*

*Dale Allen during the visit
of Hasna Sabri*

*Graham Hodge and Valera
Allen during Hasan Sabri's
visit in Swaziland.*

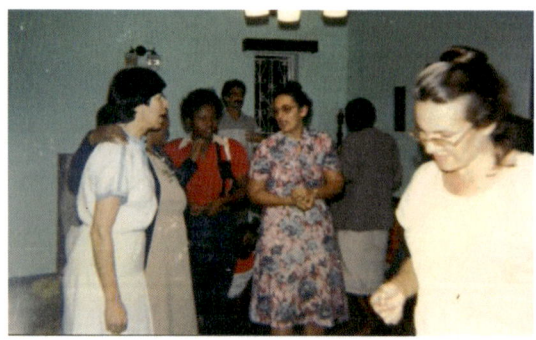

Some of the Baha'i friends during the visit of Hasan Sabri in Swazailand.(In the foreground L-R -Dr Irma Allen, Mujgand Derrakhshani and Patti Siemantel)

END OF TRAVEL TEACHING

In 1987 my days of travel-teaching ended and I started to look for work more seriously. My financial resources were exhausted. I found out that unless I was from a foreign country and bringing some expertise, there was no chance of finding work in Swaziland. I was requested to reside in Hlatikulu by the National Assembly. I found two lovely souls who accepted me as if I was part of their family. They were Lesley and Graham Hodge, both from the United Kingdom. They were Caretakers at the Baha'i Center in Hlatikulu. I had visited them in the past but now I was to see them on a daily basis.

Graham and Lesley Hodge

(L-R) Joseph, Lois, and Ruth Hodge,
children of the Hodges at a younger age .

The Baha'I Center in Hlatikulu

I stayed with them and experienced the best days of my stay in Swaziland. I had given up my rented house and sold all furniture because my girlfriend wished that I should move to the United States because of mutual employment problems. Soon, these two people had to move and was further equested to stay at the Baha'i National Center for a while. As I was living in the quarters used for children's preschool education, I had to move again, because classes had to begin in the school.. This time I met Crispin Pimberton-Piggott who offered housing at his home and a job making wire-fencing at his company. I moved to far away Siteki, where I resided until it was advisable, for purposes of obtaining a visa to enter the United States, to move back to South Africa.

Crispin and Margaret Pemberton-Piggott

TEACHING IN SWAZILAND

From the moment I arrived in Swaziland I was involved I activities: from Commemorations held at exact times at dawn , daytime, or evenings; to deepening classes; prayer meetings and teaching trips to the villages outside Manzini. While I resided in Zakhele, I had neighbors in Trelawney Park, the Dadgars who warmly invited me to their classes.

Just as I completed my travelling teaching period, a meeting was called where teaching was discussed. We were to broaden our base and teach more vigorously. Suddenly without any warning Faramarz lifted a hand and said that he was willing to offer a ride to any Swazi desiring to teach anywhere in Swaziland and on any day.It was obvious that he and Debbie had come to very amicable terms on this because there was no protest. I offered some time and had Faramarz take me around some time. Rick Ragland offered some of his time and transportation and I was able to visit Phuzumoya with him in order to teach. On the other hand, though Valera was limited in travel in those days she offered hospitality and consultation at any time of day we could get together to discuss the Faith and teaching.

My days in Swaziland were of greater growth and first inklings of independence in a foreign country, for differences between Swaziland ,and South Africa were great ,both in social life and cultural angles. I have gratitude for the Dadgar family and the Piggotts' for their support during my initial time outside of South Africa, where I had lived almost all my life. I had a taste of not only Swazi household life, but of mixed families numbering amongst them the Dadgars' who were American and Persian; the Duckers' who are American and Swazi; the Raglands' who are American and Japanese, the Carmichaels who are Colored and the Derrakhshanis' who are Persian, not to forget Canadian life in the home of the Piggott's and American in he home of he Fletcher's.. Steve and Patti Siemental were residing in Manzini,, at that tme.

Valera "Gogo" Allen with Charlotte Stirrat in Haifa Israel (1985).

Debbie Dadgar with her son Omid and Ruth Hodge, at Debbie's home.

Faramarz Dadgar at home.

A Brief Stay in Port Elizabeth

Courage was necessary

I had left South Africa in 1985 to pioneer in Swaziland and Mozambique. My departure had intended no return. However, due to an unforeseen plan to move to the United Sates, I needed a visa. This necessitated that I return to my city of birth to wait for the application for my South African documents to come through. These documents were to be compiled in my application for the visa and forwarded to the U.S. Consulate. Thus it was that I found myself in Port Elizabeth, living in my parents' house.

One afternoon I chanced to visit friends near Ferguson and Mendi Roads in New Brighton. On my way back I met a young man who was once a Baha'i. The street was very quiet and I had previously noticed that conversation was limited to mundane subjects amongst my friendsin New Brighton.. It surprised me that he did not seem to have taken care of himself as I knew him to be more orderly of dress. After greeting me the young man, who is named Motsamai Ramollo, wished to know where I had been in the past years. I replied that I had been in Swaziland. He then invited me to his home. On entering I saw his mother working frantically in the kitchen and immediately knew that something was not quite right. Normally parents greet a visitor. I kept standing as the invitation did not seem ceremonious or friendly.

Ramollo admitted that he had heard that I had visited Israel and again visited a Socialist State, as he described it. I did not dispute that because I had been to both Israel and Mozambique. He asked seriously if I knew that I could burn for that, when people did not know where my funds had come from. I became quite upset and pointed out that I had a right to spend my money any way I liked and reminded him that I was no politician. I knew at that moment that I was close to being labeled an informer and fit to be "necklaced". I felt that it was time to face up to it and state my case loudly: I said:" Ramollo, if you asked me if I were a Baha'i, you would to identify me by name, so that you have the right person, I would answer 'Yes' and if you then stated that a Baha'i believes in this that or the other and mentioned the right things, then I would say again ' Yes'. If you then said:' Robert Mazibuko, you will burn for this', I shall burn merrily knowing that I die for what I believed in, and not politics. If you will excuse me, I have to go." I opened the door and walked slowly to his gate into Mendi Road..

When I was in the street, someone followed me and asked in a low voice what the young man had wanted. I told him to go to him at his home and ask him At that point the man turned back and disappeared. I walked all the way home without mishap.

I left South Africa on October 23rd, 1987 and settled in the United States.

DEPARTURE AND VISIT

 I left the continent of Africa to marry and reside in the United States on 24th October 1987 and got married that same year on November 8th. I immediately called home after the wedding and spoke my parents to announcing the marriage to them. My little sister called me the next day to give me the marriage name to my wife, which was Nomonde(Mother of patient care). This name was from my mother. However, after my marriage, I received a letter from Esthsr Nkonzo giving another name to my wife. This letter must have been delayed for months, for it was written in 1986 while Gretchen and I were in engaged to be married. The name could not be accepted because, traditionally such a name has to be discussed by female members of the immediate family of the groom. But, Esther could not have given me a more wonderful wedding wish. I am not certain when Esther passed on, but by 2005, she was no longer in this world. This is the letter she wrote:

A NOTE FROM ESTHER SHUMIKAZI NKONZO.

" Box 15,
Mdantsnae.
17.11.86
Robert my dear son,
Alla'u'Abha

We were so glad to hear the news that you are O.K. over there. Truly, Rob, Baha'u'llah has His own plans . That is why He says: *He that giveth himself wholly to God, God shall assuredly be with him and he that placeth complete trust in God, God shall verily protect him and shield him from the wickedness of every evil plotter.*

Come home with *Makoti*, we want her. My heart even says her name should be *Nozuko* (Mother of glory)

With Baha'i love,
Shumie"

I received many letters of well-wishing from South Africa and this made me feel confirmed in my having moved.

A VISIT TO SOUTH AFRICA IN 1991

I had had a wish to visit my children for some time, but had been unable to undertake the trip because of financial concerns. I worked as a temporary help through a company, and even paying bills was not easy. However, without warning, I was offered three credit cards and accepted them. With one credit card, I secretly bought a round trip ticket to South Africa, with the intention of announcing this later. Sickness and subsequent surgery came before I was ready to talk, but this gave me an opportunity to voice my desire to my wife. The wish was accepted and preparations to depart after discharge from hospital, were accomplished easily. Since we were short of funds, I was to go alone.

THE RAGLANDS

When I visited South Africa in 1991 after being away for four years, I found that the Ma'anis' had left the area and in their place a couple of an American with a Japanese wife had moved in to pioneer. They were Rick and Yoshie Ragland. I was unable to make an appointment with them but we had met in Swaziland where they first pioneered in 1985. Rick had worked at the Baha'i World Center for some time and had later been a prominent figure at Manzini, Swaziland, where he worked for a company called *Relief Services*. The company supplied goods to a number of areas in Africa.

I could not meet with the Raglands' in Port Elizabeth because of time constraints. I had other travelling difficulties because my right arm had been bandaged with a sling after a operation on the shoulder when part of the scapula had been removed with a tumor. I tended to stay all in one place and hoped someone would visit. I was able to visit my children for short periods without tiring myself. Yoshie and Rick heard of my presence almost on the day I departed for the U.S. but they graciously found time to try, up to the time I had to be at the airport. I knew I had to go home as my wife was not in good a shape of health either. I needed to assist her too, as she had assisted me while I lay in hospital.

In 2005, I met Rick in South Africa, while he and his wife lived in Botswana. He had come on vacation, and made every effort that we meet. He pleasantly surprised me one night while I was with friends, with a visit.

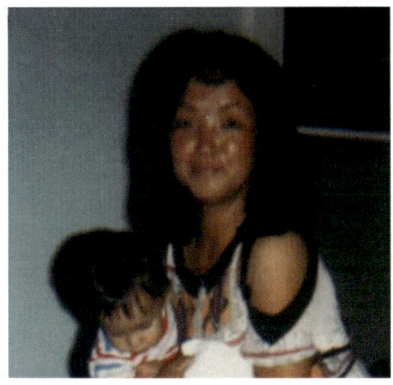

A picture of Yoshie taken during the visit of Mr Hasan Sabri in Swaziland.

A VISIT OF 1995

In 1995 I was determined to fulfill a promise to my children that I would fetch them from Africa to come and live with me in the United States. It had been eight years since I made the promise and it was time to act. I was accompanied by Gretchen who was determined to meet Faith, and gain her goodwill in taking the children from her. This stance was more acceptable in the African setting. Mothers talk to one another when it comes to children care.

I found many things had changed in the city, on my arrival. I hardly knew my way around the , but Gretchen and I went shopping for initiation blankets for my two boys who intended to go to African initiation school soon.. It was a good to see some of the old school friends in the city.

Customarily, we had to go and place stones at my parents' graves as I was away when they passed on, and I had not been able to do this with Gretchen, when I visited alone in 1991. We went together to the graveside to accomplish this act.

This time, Gretchen and I were accommodated at my younger sister's home. My sister was soon leaving to give a talk in New Zealand, as a Professor in Business Management at her university., As we had the house to ourselves, I invited my children to spend the night with us. My children were in a measure of comfort and wanted to travel with me. I had booked to take a three-day pilgrimage with Gretchen and myself. This was not to be. Their mother was unwilling to let them go. Broken hearted, I left the country.

The pioneers who were in Port Elizabeth, that time were the Anvaris. The Raglands' had left for another post.

Gretchen and Luthando in Motherwell(1995)

THE ANVARIS

When I visited Port Elizabeth in 1995, I found Mahvash and Jamshid pioneering in Port Elizabeth. There were several issues I could not resolve for them when I again visited in 2004 but then I had gone to attend my brother's funeral and could not settle into problems in any real way as I was distracted very much. I had been close to my brother in the early days and that had not left me. However, this made me feel guilty for years.

In 1995, I was able to introduce Gretchen to them and saw then genuinely entertain her as a sister. The children and I visited them in their home in Summerstrand. For this reason of trust, at a later date in 2004 they had some concerns that were beyond my ability and whose solution was out of my reach. Someday I may be able to explain my stand amicably. Let me state now that I appreciated their trust and wish for pardon for having done so little to help. That chapter remains a source of pain to both me and my wife, with whom I discussed it in detail.

Mahvash Anvari

Jamshid Anvari

Gretchen Misselt near 1989
(picture taken in Green Lake, Wisconsin.

EAST LONDON

Before leaving the country, we rented a car and travelled to East London to visit a cousin who had been so much help while I had waited for a visa. On the way we stopped at art shops and other areas:

Gretchen on the way to Mdantsane

Robert, on the way to Mdantsane

We were able to arrive at Mdantsane and meet with my three cousins, who showed my uncle's and aunts' graves, as they had recently passed on. We were also able to spend a night at the home of my cousin in Beacon Bay, East London. All in all, that was a pleasant visit.

Siphokazi Mampe, my cousin

The next day we left for Port Elizabeth and thence to Israel, for the pilgrimage and the United Kingdom to visit Graham and Lesley Hodge, my two friends I had first met at the pioneering post in Swaziland. We remembered Hlatikulu with fondness and nostalgia.

IN 1997/1998

When I was in South Africa in 1998, I had gone for the sole purpose of contacting my children and moving them to the United States. It was now eleven years since I made a solemn promise to them to fatch them to live with me , once I found housing and funds.. This time their mother was enthusiastic that they should leave with me.

All my efforts were centered on the purpose I have stated. I could not visit anybody in Port Elizabeth. I had not fully informed my siblings of my visit but chose to stay at the home of my ex-school teacher, Viola Mda, my friend of many years.

When I got to Johannesburg with the children, I received help from the National Secretary, Shohreh Rauhani and her assistant, Sylvia Benatar, in the shape of obtaining a loan from the National Assembly, through the Treasurer, David Skrenes. I have covered that story at a later stage in this book. I had envisaged staying a few days in Port Elizabeth and had prepared for just that, but found I had to be in Pretoria/Johannesburg for four weeks, while travelling papers for the children were being prepared at the U.S. Consulate; hence the appeal for a loan.

THE FINANCIAL ARRANGEMENT

It was arranged that I would receive funds which I would pay back, when the time came. Since this was a sizeable amount, these funds would be held in a bank , and released , as need came, by Sylvia Benatar, the Clerk to the National Secretary each time , until exhausted. This was in such a cordial manner and worked smoothly throughout the process of applying for visas.

Sylvia Benatar

DOCTOR DONALD MAZIBUKO'S FUNERAL , 2004

Donald passed on suddenly of a stroke in east London where he worked at the Frere and Cecilia Makiwane Hospitals as a Gynecologist. Before I could hear from family, a friend, Ronald Fudu, contacted me by email to break the news. I confirmed this by calling my cousin Sipokazi Mampe who lives in East London. While I was on my way to the funeral I stopped at my son, Emeric's home to find that I had email from my little sister, letting me know of the time, place and date of the funeral and also asking me write an obituary. By the late hour I got to the funeral, a friend had written one and presented it to the family. I accepted that too, just as the family had..

I was amazed to hear *Amazing Grace* sung in English at the funeral but not too surprised since my brother was a kind of activist. Also the service was conducted with both a white and a black priest in attendance.

Several school friends I had met in Fort hare earlier were present and had travelled from far away towns: Queenstown, Fort Beaufort and of course the surrounds of Port Elizabeth and East London.

My family(L-R)
Wandile Mazibuko;
Thobeka Melane;
Kholekile Mazibuko,
Noxolo Mazibuko

Dr Zin Jiya and his wife,
Dr Angelinah Jiya , were present
at the funeral where the picture
was taken by the author

PORT ELIZABETH, AFTER A FUNERAL

When the funeral of my brother was over, a friend who was returning home, drove me to Port Elizabeth, where I stayed in my little sister's house . It was a joy to be invited by the Muhajirs who now lived in Summerstrand, Port Elizabeth, to spend a evening being entertained by their family. This came as a relief after the sadness of the funeral. These were Baha'i friends I had valued so much, since their school days in Johannesburg. It was also at this time that I went to visit Cowan in order to enquire of a computer project they said they were planning. I was introduced to their new library and computer room. They needed computers and wished I could help. On returning to the United States, I found this project so complex and involving that I decided to postpone commencing to even find donors. The project is still being considered but was further discouraged by a break-in and theft at the school, as was reported by the principal.

THE MUJAJIRS

Muhajir family on Baha'i Pilgrimage in Haifa, Israel. (picture taken with the Shrine of the Bab in the background)

I met Sepi Rouhani and Abbas Muhajir in Johannesburg when they attended school at the University of the Witwatersrand. Sepi was in the Social Sciences and continued to earn a Doctorate, while Abbas became an Engineer.

142

At the time I met them, they were not married but knew each other very well. I spent an evening with them after dinner at Abbss and Sepi's home and we recalled old days..

Abbas had been a keen basketball player and great at strategic planning..He and Mehran had been able to keep me in their apartment in Johannesburg for weeks in 1987 , so that I could give a talk to interested students, on Baha'i subjects.

At a certain point, when I had left the country, they, Sepi and Abbas , decided to pioneer in Port Elizabeth as a couple. It filled me with joy to note that they chose to live in Summerstrand where I had learned to be a Baha'I through Rosemary and Emeric Sala in the sities. Mehran had also moved into the vicinity of Summerstrand though I never visited his home.

Sepi Rauhani taught as a Professor at the Nelson Mandela Metropolitan University where she met my little sister, Dr Noxolo Mazibuko, and befriended her. While Abbas's work put him in a situation of constant travel, sometimes outside the country, Sepi took up the work of deepening the youth. However, the constant separation eventually caused both of them to move to a country where they could live in closer proximity and with less disturbance to the union.

Sepi, left , Abbas and Jamshid Anvari with some of the African friends in Port Elizabeth (a gift from Sepi)

The Muhajirs loved beauty.
These are the surroundings
they lived in.

During the time the Muhajirs' were in Port Elizabeth, Sepi encouraged me to send some Writings to the youth of Port Elizabeth from the United States. I have sent Writings to them every Baha'i occasion including Baha'i Holy Days since that invitation..

Here is an example of what I send:

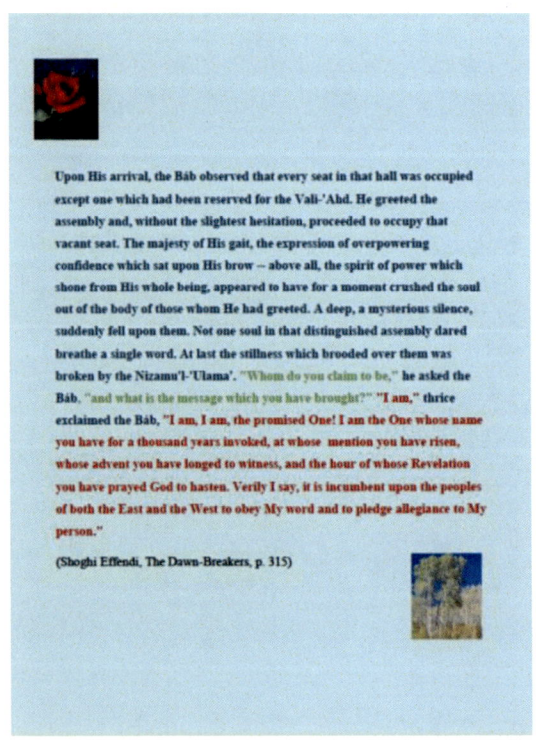

This was on the occasion
of the Commemoration
of the Birth of the Bab:

Mehran Muhajir with a youth group in Port Elizabeth

A Visit of 2005

JOHANNESBURG

 I cannot call the time I spent in South Africa in 2004 a visit, as I had gone there to attend the funeral of my younger brother who had passed on suddenly. I was, therefore, too distracted and out of focus and could not interact very well. However, some good things happened in East London where my brother is buried and later in Port Elizabeth. I met a number of my college friends from Fort hare who had come to pay respects at the funeral.

In 2005, I went for another visit, this time not in grief. I decided to visit my friends, the Hodges' in York, the Baha'i Center in Johannesburg and spend some time in Cape Town , before meeting with family in Port Elizabeth. Gretchen who was coming later, would meet me in Cape Town and we would then proceed together home to Port Elizabeth , at which point she would go back to the U.S.A. I have told the story of my visit to York in the book *This Side Up*, but there are some stories I have not told about the Baha'i Center and Cape Town. Those will be told in this book.

On returning to Heathrow Airport from York, I found great difficulty in finding the boarding terminal for South Africa. I found I had to be on a ride by train to get there. It reminded me of a time I had in Atlanta when I had to eventually walk the distance. I had noticed on an earlier visit that the airport in Johannesburg had changed; however, I had no difficulty finding an exit and a place to wait. I was driven immediately to the new Baha'i Center. I found out this Center was in a new area and was far larger than the Center we had on Rustenburg Road, in Melville. There is room for more offices and the Archives' Office where Lowell and Edith worked is large.

My friend, Lowell Johnson, at the new Baha'i Center (2005)

A view of the Baha'i National Center in Johannesburg

A view of the Baha'i National Center in Johannesburg

A view of the Baha'i National Center in Johannesburg

CAPE TOWN

Since I had to touch all the areas I had in mind, in the following days I moved to Cape Town. I was met by Tahirih Matthee, who welcomed me in her home. Gretchen and I had been assigned a bedroom.

Tahirih Matthee, Baha'i National Director of External Affairs, at her home.

When Gretchen arrived, in a few days, Tahirih and I met her.

A VISIT TO THE MARKS'

In the very short time we had we were able to spend an evening with Geoff, Amy and Bahiyyih Marks , at their home. It was very pleasant to see Geoff again because I had last seen him in Wilmette, Illinois. In fact, on my very first year in the United States , Geoff had invited me on a trip to Beloit, Wisconsin,, where he gave a slide show on Africa. The Marks' family has now moved to Israel to serve at the Baha'i World Center. It was a joy to be in their house later in Haifa, Israel early in 2009.

A FEAST AT TAHIRIH AND GREGORY'S HOME

We later attended the Feast of Power(Qudrat) at the Matthees' and the Gallows'(They live on almost the same building.The Gallows'. Gakkie and Jasmine are Tahirih's parents). Geoff was present at the Feast.

Gretchen, Gakkie and Nabil Rasiet, at the Baha'i Feast in Cape Town.

Nabil Rasiet and Geoff Marks at the Baha'i Feast in Cape Town

PORT ELIZABETH

Gretchen and I reached Port Elizabeth at the time of our 18th wedding anniversary. My relatives celebrated this with a small barbecue in the backyard of my elder sister's home on the 8th November . The twins, Roselyn and Dr Rosemond Mazibuko , my sisters daughters got busy preparing for the barbecue or *braaivleis.*

Roselyn Mazibuko

Dr Rosemond Mazibuko

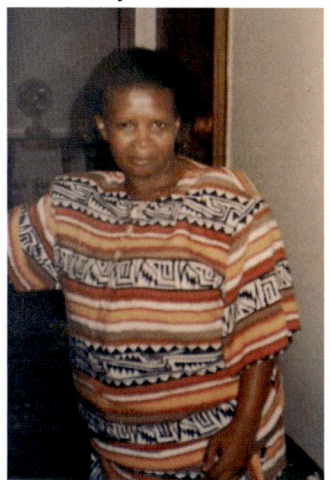 

(My elder sister's twins)

THE COMMEMORATION OF THE BIRTHDAY OF BAHA'U'LLAH

On the 12th November Gretchen and I were invited to a party commemorating the Birth of Baha'u'llah, where some introductions were made and we were asked to address the meeting in both English and Xhosa, for the benefit of the younger participants. Before the meeting, I had to have my pants altered by Gretchen. My sister watched with joy.

Gretchen sewing my pants at my sister's home in Port Elizabeth in preparation for going out.

Preparations for the occasion of commemorating the Birthday of Baha'u'llah in Port Elizabeth

Hailey and Malibongwe Fudu,
entertaining the participants
with a song

VISITING AND ENTERTAINING OLD FRIENDS

Gretchen and I were able to visit Faith Kato-Nonyati in Motherwell, my home at Msimka, New Brighton, have lunch with my younger brother, Wandile at Ferguson Road, New Brighton, and one night we went to see an old friend of my family, a retired Hospital Tutor, Nosidima Sishi in Kwamagxaki.

Gretchen left for the U.S.A at this point, in consideration of her animals which were left either kernelled or with neighbors. I stayed on another two weeks and visited with two friends and Viola Mda.

Mfiki Osmond Nkumba
a childhood friend.

155

Mxolisi Cumngce Gawe, whom I worked with at the hospital and whose brother, Stephen, I had met in Fort Hare University.

BAHA'IS IN SOUTHERN CAPE

APPOINTMENTS AND ELECTIONS
OF BAHA'IS FROM EASTERN CAPE

 The first Baha'i from the Eastern Cape to serve on the National Spiritual Assembly of South Africa was Rosemary Sala. Rosemary had already served on a National Assembly, the first in Canada. The election in South Africa occurred in 1968 before she left for Canada and later pioneered in Mexico. There followed the appointment of Robert Mazibuko as National Xhosa Translator and as a Travelling Teacher. There were several other Travelling Teachers ,in the Eastern Cape, including,Beaty Kato, Joyce Dwashu, Esther Nkonzo, Reinette Ndubaza and Cynthia Ngodwane. Joyce Dwashu served on the National Assembly in the mid- eighties. The travelling teachers in the Eastern Cape that are mentioned above also served on the National Assembly of the Ciskei when it was formed in 1985.

In 1974 Rose Gates served on the National Assembly followed by Robert Mazibuko in 1975.At this time Pumeza Simane from Mdantsane , served on the National Youth Committee. From Port Elizabeth, Angelinah Gcume was also appointed to the same National Youth Committee, replacing Nanette Tlome, who served for a year.

In the eighties, Eghbal served on the National Teaching Committee and Ronald Fudu on the National Consolidation Committee.

In the past year two young people from Port Elizabeth have been invited to serve a Youth Year of Service at the Baha'i World Center. They are Nolitha Mangisa and Bayan Gcume.

PROGRESS IN COMMUNITIES OF BAHA'IS

Today the whole area of Port Elizabeth is under one Baha'i Local Spiritual Assembly because all the townships fall under one municipality and civil boundaries have changed. This comes at a time when the Baha'is are used to Baha'i Administration as well as teaching the Faith on their own. The friends are now free to use the halls and facilities in the city for their meetings.

When I left in 1985, there was one pioneer, Tammy Conklin, who was a student at Rhodes University, in Grahamstown but she has since moved out.

A frequent visitor to Port Elizabeth was Dr Michael walker. He had learned enough Xhosa to relate well with the Africans in the area. In his quiet way Mike is a great teacher of the Faith and was of assistance in taking teaching trips to Mdantsane and the Transkei. During Conventions he was prepared to take a car-load to the meeting, either from cape Town or Port Elizabeth..

When they were completing building the Center in Cape Town, I arrived to attend Summer School to find Mike Walker in his shorts wrestling a concrete cutter, slicing the slabs that paved the yard of the Center. This is one example of what I knowof him and I an certain that he would be embarrassed if he heard me say these things about him or try to minimize talking about himself but I am doing the writing at the moment.

Of course John Agulhas was always there with his songs and guitar, visiting both Port Elizabeth and Mdatsane.; while Marvel Gray visited and kept in touch throughout the community building process.

The Huevel family with Dr Michael walker in cape Town.

A group of Baha'is with members of the National Spiritual Assembly of South Africa at the home of one of the local Baha'is in Port Elizabeth.

One year the National Assembly had a meeting in Port Elizabeth.

In 2005 the Commemoration of the Birth of Baha'u'llah was held in a hall in the city. In the foreground (front row), are Ronal Fudu, Robert Mazibuko, Gretchen Misselt and Ivy Gcume.

Robert Mazibuko with Ronald Fudu hosting a religious program at the radio station in Port Elizabeth.

The local Baha'is have an arrangement with the South African Broadcasting Corporation whereby each week they host a service on a radio channel.

Ephens Senne of Pretoria on the left, back row, Shelley Cook(back row extreme right, and Vuyelwa Mbotya (front row right) were all in Evanston, IL, after attending a World Congress in New York, NY.

In 1992 a World Congress was held in New York, the City of the Covenant of the Baha'is to commemorate the hundredth year after the Ascension of Baha'u'llah. After the congress many Baha'is visited friends in the States, and so that evening some came to our apartment in Evanston, IL . Gilbert and Tabitha Tombisa of Pretoria also arrived to spend an evening and left the next morning.

Nolitha Mangisa who now works at the National Center in Johannesburg, South Africa, has moved to the Baha'I World Center, Haifa , Israel.

Ronald and Grace Fudu took pilgrimage to Haifa, Israel

Bayan Gcume , now at the Baha'i World Center.

BROUGHT UP AS A BAHA'I: NEXT GENERATION

Since the seventies, and even earlier, there have been many children who have been brought up in Baha'i families. At this time, these children are grown up. As proof of the childhood of some of their, pictures are provided:

Emeric visiting in Umtata (Picture by his father)

Angelinah Gcume, now a school teacher, served on the National Youth Committee for several years, travelling to Johannesburg for meetings each month. (Photographer unknown)

Malibongwe Fudu with his sister
Lunathi, as a teenager
(Picture by author)

Malibongwe with his wife Hailey, a lady from California.
They now have two children

Malibongwe Vahid Fudu who was born in the seventies, became an Engineer and married a school teacher from California, Hailey Fudu . They have settled in Durban with their two children, Tajalli and Dayyan.

Tajalli and baby brother , Dayyan Fudu.

Emeric Husayn Bonga and his brother William Jusuf Luthando, both born in the seventies, moved to the United States in 1998.

Lunathi Fudu, the youngest child of Grace and Roanld Fudu , is completing her university education in Port Elizabeth

Nomakhwezi Tahirih Fudu the eldest daughter of Grace and Ronald grew up to serve in Baha'i Diplomatic environment.

Nomakhwezi Fudu

SOME STORIES TO REMEMBER

The Skrenes' Family of Durban

David and Rosalee Skrenes at Green lake, Wisconsin (By author)

 It is a mistake not to tell how I met and became friends with the Skrenes' family. This is because I came to be closely related with this family. I met first Bryan who was a Medical student when he was appointed to the National Youth Committee, but I did not get to know much about him except that he was thorough secretary of that committee. Then one National Convention held at Umgababa (Umgababa is a holiday resort near the coast), I chanced to take a moment off from babysitting my son, Bomga Emeric, who was with me. I took a short walk to the beach. On the beach was a young blond girl who sat sadly, perhaps contemplating. I felt I should say a word. It was so unusual to see a lonely figure on the beach during a Convention. She introduced herself as Dana Skrenes.

I am not certain when the next encounter with another member of the Skrenes family ,occurred but I do know what I said to her. She had on a sweater which was very wooly (I guess this was in winter). She had her head sticking out of the wooly sweater like a sheep. I immediately told her that she looked like a "Lamb" and the name stuck on my mind. I learned that her name was Teresa or was it Theresa? I had been reading about Marie Therese in French and compared it to Maria Theresa of Russia. At any rate that was her name. I became friends with and met her every time I went to meetings in Johannesburg.

In those days my health was none too good and everyone began to notice. I would so distraught at my home at times, that I would find solace in calling the Skrenes family at odd times of the day and they would answer. I would sometimes speak to the Lamb. One night I called and asked if the "Lamb" was in and was told she was out. I then asked if it was the boy/girl scene and David answered:"..Something like that …!" By that time I had learned that David and Roselee were the parents in the Skrenes' family.

Early in 1984 I had a discussion with my children and found out that they deplored the fact that they were not permitted to live with me as I was married a second time. Promising to find solutions, I then decided to go on pilgrimage to clarify my thoughts. While on pilgrimage I met Gretchen. I noticed that she had children and just loved the way she took care of them and how she related to both of them. Somehow that friendship got enhanced into a firmer commitment.

At the next Assembly meeting in Johannesburg, I handed the *halva* I had bought in Haifa, during pilgrimage, to the members of the National Assembly. At tea break, that day, I met Teresa and decided I would talk to her, perhaps for the last. I met her in the hallway as she hurried to her meeting and said to her:

"Teresa, you and I had a good thing going, but we had a problem… age" and she said ;':It does not matter because you called me a 'Lamb' and that is important. "

I later reminded her that Lambs do get sacrificed sometimes. Teresa went on to marry Ludfi Noor who was serving on another National Committee which met at the same time and they moved to first Kwazulu and later to the United States.

I moved first to Swaziland and later to the United States where I married Gretchen. We are a group of very good friends. Bryan Skrenes married a Persian lady who is a doctor in the Social Sciences and moved to Canada. Larry

Skrenes, another son, married Ruhiyyih (Gallow), a cousin of Ludfi's and moved to the United States.

Larry Skrenes and son

Ludfi Noor in later years in the United States

Larry and Ruhiyyih Skrenes At the House of Worship in Wilmette, IL

Drs Bryan and Laleh Skrenes

I NOTICED YOUR SON

In the early eighties, I realized that I did not know enough about my son who lived away from me. I arranged for us to go together on a long train-trip to be acquainted. We went to Convention by train.

Luthando Mazibuko at the National Convention

When the Convention was concluded I spent time with my younger brother who was a Gynecologist in Durban. During the course of that visit I touched on David at the I.B.M. offices in the city.

I had not brought many toys with me, so my son had a stick he was playing with. It was curious to notice that this stick could: crawl on the ground like a car; shimmy up a tree, and fly like an airplane. I pointed out this behavior to David in a worried attitude. David laughed and said:"Leave him alone, He is an artist!". Years later this was confirmed by a friend, Mthembu while I was in the States.

Mthembu and Ivy Gcume conducted many children's classes, perhaps because they had many children of relatives living with hem. Thembu advised that Luthando be placed on an Art Program because he drew a picture of everything he saw. Today Luthando is an Illustrator.

A PROMISE FULFILLED: FRIENDSHIP PROVED

At this point , it is necessary to explain the assistance performed by the Skrenes' family in helping two Africans from the Eastern Cape to emigrate to the United States in 1998and thus aid a father fulfill a promise.. This is done in consideration of the poor state of affairs of the Skrenes' family at the time it rendered the service to a friend. This unfortunate circumstance was unknown to those who received the help until recently. It was kept silent. There were facts about the Skrenes family that I did not know about. These were supplied by Rosalee and David when we met at the Green Lake Conference in 2011, some thirteen years later. We attend this conference annually.

The Skrenes' family had come to South Africa from the United States and settled in the Natal area of South Africa. They had been a large family of nine, but at the time in question, many of the children were married. Not only were the children married, but they had married into Malay and Persian families in South Africa.

As it later transpired, at this time of emigration David Skrenes, the husband, had just had brain surgery and his wife, Rosalie was taking charge of family affairs.. However, David was also the Treasurer of the National Assembly of South Africa.

The two emigrants, Emeric and Luthando Mazibuko were caught in Johannesburg, without enough funds to apply for visas or for a prolonged stay in that area of Pretoria while waiting for documents. Their father was with them but had provided for a stay of a few days instead of an undetermined period of more than four weeks which he was going to be forced to stay with them. This was all necessary that he remain with the children , but unfortunate and difficult to bear that he could not independently support them.

An appeal for funds was made by the three Africans to the National Assembly. The appeal was transmitted to David Skrenes. David, unable to act, indicated to Rosalie to grant the request and the funds were made immediately available to the three in Johannesburg.

That year, David, unable to give the National Report at the National Convention, could no longer be expected to function as Treasurer in the following year. The family finally moved back to the United Sates. However, even there, they appear at Conferences and other events.

During that four-week stay in the Johannesburg area, the emigrants and their father enjoyed the welcome hospitality of the Tombisas' who were unobtrusive but offered what they had in terms of maintenance and some privacy. When it was time to go, the Tombisas' with Sam Von Eck quietly arranged transportation to the airport.

Gilbert and Thabitha Tombisa during the Jubilee Celebrations

THE STATUS OF THE TWO YOUNGSTERS

*Emeric and Kraren Maz-
ibuko getting married three
years after Emeric's arrival
in the United States*

*Luthando Mazibuko graduat-
ing seven years after arrival
in the United States.*

WE OWE HER GRATITUDE TOO!

The two children soon got acquainted with life in the United States. Emeric found work, got married, had his first child and graduated from university. Luthando attended high school, got his GED while employed part time, got his Associates Degree, moved to study at the school where his stepmother worked, and studied , and graduated in a B.A. He went on to get his Master's. What surprised me is the ease with which Luthando managed to study right through hhis university on scholarships. This fact made life much easier for me. All I had to do was act as the taxi from school to work, and back home. Karen, Emeric's partner, was a great help to Emeric in giving advice and sta-bilizing him through the early years.

In all, this is how much the Skenes' and Tombisa families assisted in my finding some peace of mind and in establishing credibility for a father in dis-tress. Italia Penelope Tombisa, was instrumental in finding us a place at her parent's home. In as much as she was employed at the U.S. Consulate, at the time, we looked forward to seeing her each we went for a visa appointment. We feel we owe her a vote of thanks and undying gratitude for her assistance..

Italia Penelope Tombisa, who housed me and my children at her parents' home in Eersterust, Pretoria, while we waited for my children's visas to enter the United States

A STORY OF A LONELY MAN

To my knowledge, David had never lived or visited Port Elizabeth but he was good company while I looked for opportunities of pioneering in the Transkei. I often visited him but found him a quiet man. David was a teacher at Theko Vocational school in 1979. He had a great interest in African culture but soon found that he had to step back and digest what he knew I understood that he moved to Malaysia where he served on the Baha'i Administration. For many hears, no news were received of him.

I received David's address while I was in the United States from one of the Baha'i friends. He had pioneered in the Transkei and in Swaziland for some years:

"Hey Robert!
Kunjalo!
Kunjan'ekhaya?
Kunjani bantfwana?

I am writing to say happy holidays (though I guess we are not taking Ayyam-i-Ha off, are we) and to give you David Garcia's address. It is stateside these days in northern California or southern Oregon - sort of moving around a bit. He just found out he is eligible for all sorts of things because he is an old warhorse or something. That is really funny because he is a warrior in the spiritual army!

I am back in Swaziland for a few days after returning from Mozambique. I seem to have landed myself a position with a program for biomass energy conservation that involves travel and design and doing good. www.probec.org might have a little info on what I do, but basically it is designing and creating the production of improved cooking stoves for the masses in various countries. It is of course really challenging to get things manufactured in Maputo and Lusaka etc etc.

New Dawn Engineering survives barely and will pass to the staff pretty soon - hopefully in March, you never know...

Margaret is in Waterloo Ontario and enjoying working for RIM the people that make the BlackBerry. Funnily enogh she is in the engineering department.

Jeremy is way up in the control of manufacturing of motherboards at a company called Celestica in Toronto. He is in charge of robotic inspection systems and without him I think they would collapse. Man, big companies are a stupid bunch. Anyway....

Nigel and Desmond are in Macau this week for the annual pioneers to China get-together. They live in Dalian in the far east near N Korea. Both are reasonably well considering they are living in China. Desmond works for Dell running their servers for Asia-Pacific.

And that's the whole story I guess. I am sitting in the factory where I now live typing in the heat. Been a hot year.

Best regards
Crispin in Matsapha"

This was Crispin Pemberton-Piggott, writing from Swaziland.

From that moment I was able to reconnect with David, I soon learned that David was a veteran of the Vietnamese War. At this time he was in the Philippines and not well. His life was one of great pain until he passed on in Mexico after having lived in Hawaii also. I kept in touch with him and he answered diligently. Here is some of the correspondence:

CORRESPONDENCE WITH DAVID GARCIA FROM THE UNITED STATES:

"March 6, 2007.
Dear David,

In order to open up all lines of communication to us from you, I shall give you my address, as well as my future address:

2644 N 3501st Road

Marseilles

Illinois 61341.

And

1739 Michigan Road

Washington Island

WI 54246

We do not use the telephone much as we rely on prepaid telephones. As it were, we cannot spend much, because we are both on social security.

My wife goes by the name of Gretchen Misselt but has an African name of Nomonde given by my late mother.

I use also two other email addresses:

RMazibuko@hotmail.com

RMazibuko@bahaiemail.com

I like writing letters with graphics and pictures but am not sure if you use the MAC or PC. I use the PC."

"Re: Contact again

Tuesday, June 12, 2007 5:30 PM
From:

"Robert Mazibuko" <mazibukorfk@yahoo.com>
View contact details

To:

"David Garcia" <drgarcia9@email.com>

Dave,

I am sorry to hear of your suffering. I do know what you mean by pleasant, unfeeling people, I have lived with them, especially in the work environment.I wish I were nearer to offer some nursing service. It has become so difficult to even communicate these days, because everything foreign is suspect. I shall pray that you find some patience through this test. Remember the opportunities of service you found in Africa and be grateful. Do not worry about being away from home and friends. Think of the African idiom that a man's grave is next to the road. I shall mention your name to the friends on the island when we pray so that they can think of you. Remember also the Hand of the Cause Mr Sears. At the end of a talk he would say:"Remember me in your prayers"

With much love and appreciation,

Robert Mazibuko"

"David Garcia <drgarcia9@gmail.com> wrote:

Hi, Robert!

I'm happy you've made the move to your island in Wisconsin. Am recovering from a serious cancer attack that just about helped me graduate to the next world. (I never would have believed that such pain exists.) A wonderful couple, (a doctor born in Egypt with his Jewish-American nurse wife), went through a lot of trouble to get me the anti-testosterone implant required for my survival over the next few months as well as the medication to deal with the pain and weakness.

I find that i can cope with cancer much better when i don't have unloving white women with huge feminist egoes (that are never wrong, that never need to apologize, etc.) to deal with. So, today i put two more email addresses of such women on my blocked (filtered) list. It makes life more peaceful. (And believe it or not, these woman are actually still chasing me — a sick old man! — as though we were in high school. It never occurs to them that one should be nice and pleasant in order to attract another.)

My memory is not very good these days. Did i tell you that

i'm no longer in Hawaii (or Oregon or California) and am now back in Mexico?

I hope all is well with you!

Cheer!
david"

Hi, dear brother Robert!

After all this time i'm finally sending you a reply to your wonderful and most artistic and sincere letter with pictures. It's attached here.

With very warmest Baha'i love and good wishes to you, Robert!

david

A LETTER WITH NO ANSWER

This is a letter I wrote to David Garcia, which reached his address after his passing. So it never had an answer. This is an example of the letters I wrote him at that time.

(This letter is slightly edited for clarity but most of it remains as it was sent)

" 1739 Michigan Road,
Washington Island, WI 54246.
July 25, 2007.
Dave,
I watched a documentary of the rescue of hostages in Sierra Leon and could not help but think of those days of anxiety in Southern Africa. We still have many loyalties from those days and they will last to the next world. In the midst of tribulations, I read in the Writings that when we have tribulations and trials,

we have to be thankful. Others do not have this precious gift of being chosen for trial by Him. Nothing happens but s recorded in His presence. On another day I found a program about the theory of parallel universes and was pleasantly surprised that science has now totaled eleven universes in which we live. I had seen this prayer earlier:

Immeasurably exalted art Thou, O Lord! Protect us from what lieth in front of us and behind us, above our heads, on our right, on our left, below our feet and every other side to which we are exposed. Verily, Thy protection over all things is unfailing.[1]

Compilations, Baha'i Prayers, p. 133)

Ye are better known to the inmates of the Kingdom on high than ye are known to your own selves. Think ye these words to be vain and empty? Would that ye had the power to perceive the things your Lord, the All-Merciful, doth sec things that attest the excellence of your rank, that bear witness to the greatness of your worth, that proclaim the sublimity of your station! God grant that your desires and unmortified passions may not hinder you from that which hath been ordained for you.

(Compilations, Baha'i World Faith, p. 118)

When we arrive we surely shall have a story to tell. In the mean time, we must endure what he has set for us. So, instead of showing tears , I shall endeavor to show joy…

A week ago, we had a jazz band from the mainland .It was composed of very young guys , the youngest of whom could have been seventeen or eighteen. They attempted some good numbers like "Billy's Jump", "Blue Monk". The pianist played something between the Wynton Kelly and Red Garland style. Some of them were from Illinois, Louisiana, Wisconsin. It was nice to hear them and remember the song that "All God's children got rhythm" , but I tried to find their message and decided that they were still too young to have a message I could relate to. I guess age has her own each time she comes around.

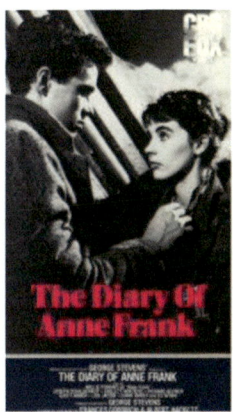

We enjoyed watching a play based on the "Diary of Anne Frank" by some island actors. It was quite good because it portrayed the lives of the family while in hiding but did not remove the danger they lived in and their predicament. I could appreciate this very much because as a Baha'i, living under the political and religious conditions of the time, I received much assistance and understanding from the Jewish community. It also helped , at the time, that my mother worked for a Jewish family.

— The Bab"

You probably will be surprised at my reaction to Cajun Music .I attended a concert of a group from the mainland who brought Cajun Music to the island. I enjoyed some of it but had my reservations.

These are not really bad musical instruments but their sound is very reminiscent of conditions in South Africa under the Afrikaner influence. I have learned to reconcile myself with the situation by citing that New York was once called "New Amsterdam"! However, I do realize that even the Dutch East India Company would be shocked to know that there has been such progress!

Before leaving South Africa , I told an Afrikaner guy that I was marrying a Scandinavian girl in the States and he replied that I was going to become his brother-in-law!

I can now believe it because this is the Norwegian dress, very close to the Dutch dress..

I spent some time reviewing Lowell's war-time scrap book while he did what he will always do , entertain you and cook meals for you.

Lowell does what Xhosas call "eating with an old chalice". This means that one is old and still going.

Some time ago, I heard a nightingale sing in Paris and I had heard one sing earlier while I was in Israel.

May the Nightingale of Paradise sing you the sweetest of melodies, far sweeter than can be depicted.

I felt that it would not hurt to give you accompaniment.

Best of this life and beyond,
    Robert Mazibuko"

I could include more correspondence from David, but I feel that this would suffice.

David Garcia

CATASTROPHIC DEATH IN MDANTSANE

Though there were things I needed to find out and did not, there was one thing I did pursue for some years. I wished to visit the grave of three Baha'is who had been murdered in Mdantsnae and buried in East London. Jamshid, whose brother, Hushmand was one of the three , and Mahvash , Jamshid's wife, tried so hard to get me a contact in East London who could direct me,. However, the plan failed. It was in 2004 that Ronald Fudu drove me to East London and showed me the desired resting place. I found that they were buried in the same tomb, took some pictures and said prayers for the progress of the three in the Next World.

*The resting place of the three martyrs of Mdantsane
(Riaz, Shamam and Husmand) executed at the Baha'i
Center during a Baha'i gathering.*

186

There were some unworthy words inscribed on a wall in Port Elizabeth but I shall not dwell on that, because I understand the stance of the Persian Baha'is of accepting death in the service of the Faith as a worthy assistance to the growth of that Faith. Part of the reason for my concern was that I had been friends with Shamam since his school days, and had met Riaz and Razi Razavi on their arrival in South Africa. The arrival of Riaz and Razi had posed a problem for the South African government because Riaz was of a darker completion than Razi, and according to the law, they could not settle in the same residential area. The National Assembly advised them to settle in the nearby free African countries. Riaz had been able to settle in the Ciskei once that homeland attained independence. Shamam's story is told in the book

This Side Up (Mazibuko, 2010).

However accepting we are concerning these deaths, it is still a mystery how these three could be singled out in Mdantsnae, where the Faith was known by so many. Rose Gates had made certain that the name of the Faith was noised abroad in all Eastern Cape. By this time she was no longer in that vicinity, but her name and religion remained amongst her many friends..

Dr Shamam Bakhshandeghi

The letters written by Shamam were forwarded to a member of the Universal House of Justice who replied that they were worth holding in the Archives because of his sudden death and the circumstances surrounding that death.

SOME STORIES ON TRAVEL-TEACHING

Most of the teaching of the Faith in the Eastern Cape and the Cape Midlands was accomplished through travel teaching. Each travelling teacher has many stories of experiences in the teaching field. Some of these stories may have to do with getting lost while searching for believers in a locality. Being lost at night is perhaps understandable and very dangerous, but one can get lost in broad daylight. I have done this spiritually and physically. Here are a few stories:

WANDERING AND WONDERING

At the beginning of 1970 I was in Johannesburg. I knew just about two places to go to outside of the street I lived on in Phefeni, Soweto; I knew the Baha'i Center and how to catch a train home. I did so wish to visit other areas in the big city. One morning I had a moment to spare and I went exploring. I was so fascinated with what I saw that I lost track of time and distance before realizing that I did not know my ay back to the railway station. By this time , I had learned to be very selective of where one asks for directions, therefore, I kept quiet and got lost even more. I knew no one in the city , and was quite on my own, however, I marched with the confidence of one with no care in the world. Actually I was frightened and did not wish to find myself in that predicament by dusk. I did not have the telephone number of the Center and was at a loss as to how this would unfold.

Quite by chance, in my wandering, I came upon a marketplace. It was the busiest place I had seen in the city, with a great number of Africans around. I dared not ask even one even though I knew I was looking for 23 Rustenburg Road. I moved around from stall to stall of goods for sale, without buying anything.

Suddenly, I noticed a very bust taxi rank. It was already the afternoon of the day and I wished to be on ground I recognized. I walked slowly to one of the taxis and told the driver to take me to 23 Rustenburg Road. I did not know how much this was going to cost me , but decided to figure that out when I got there. Apparently, Rustenburg Road was not such a well-known street, for the driver went out to ask someone where such a street was. I still do not know how he got to Rustenburg Road, but became aware that the driver was asking me to look out for the house I was going to. It appeared that house numbers were hidden. Three things helped me find the Center. One was that the house was amongst some trees in the front; the walls near the hedge were made of stone masonry and old; and the driveway had black gravel on it, it was not paved. As we cruised down the street, I saw all three signs and asked the driver to stop. The fare was a whole R4.75, and fortunately I had that much on me. I got down and, to my surprise, found I was right. I reported his incident and was asked to do some work to pay back the fare as this was all travel teaching pocket money. I worked for some minutes and this was soon forgotten. I was only grateful but guilty..

MAGUSHENI

Late in 1969 I was in the Transkei searching for the village of Magusheni. This village is in the area of Pondoland. The area was not known for its particular kindness in population. I had covered the distance from Mt Ayliff to Mfundisweni on foot, reaching Mfundisweni at night. Fortunately, a family took pity of me and took me in for the night, under very strict rules. After a night of discomfort, I was directed to a bus which in turn dropped me off at a junction I had seen on the map; from there I took a Railway bus to Magusheni. On arrival I was not sure I had even reached my destination, because there was no building in sight. On asking for directions, which was ridiculous, as Magusheni was all around where I stood, the bus station was pointed out.

I had a list of names and a name of a school. However, it was December and schools were not open. The direction of the school was pointed and I trusted that someone would know a name near to the school. However no one volunteered any information. After walking for hours I found I was not far to Mfundisweni where I came from! I turned back and found two men conversing. One of them pointed to a hill where a man on horseback had stopped. He said near the man on horseback was the house I was looking for. Like a fool I travelled towards the hill. On reaching the foot of the hill, I was amazed that the man on horseback was gone! However, I travelled on.

By sunset, I was still looking. In the dark, a young man decided to help. The house I sought was no more than about a mile from where I was and I must have passed the house many times as it was hidden behind a hill.

I was welcomed as if I was a long lost brother, which was in a way true. The lady in the house, a Ms Mahlaba, gave me hot water to bathe my feet and a hot cup of tea before inviting me to supper. It turned out that she had seen me in Durban earlier that year! There was no real need for me to teach as she was doing all the teaching in that area and seemed quite capable. All I could do was ask about the wellness of the Baha'i community, only to be assured that all was in order and the address list was up to date.. The next morning I packed my tote bag and moved out by bus, this time to a town I actually knew. Only to find that I had to go into an hotel as the continuing bus did not run on Sundays. I was in Kokstad heading for Mt Frere. It is difficult to be lost in a place where the only address there is either the Post Office; a trading store or a school! This was the case in the Transkei in those days.

GET IGNORED

Once I had settled to teach in the Cape Town area known as the cape Peninsula. While visiting in Mossel Bay, I sustained an injury and had to go back to Cape Town for a short vacation of about a week. I was residing in Lansdowne and had taken a bus from there. I had no problem finding the railway station in the city and wandering around Cape Town city was very pleasant if not uncomfortable for the congestion.

At sunset I headed for the railway station, hoping to ask somebody there for the bus number back to Lansdowne. I asked a Colored ticket examiner for directions and he just about rudely ignored me. I guessed that, even in Cape Town, Friday night was no time to be asking questions in the streets.

It took me hours to find a bus back as sunset in the midweek is no time to ask for directions from workers as they headed home. When I did get to Lansdowne, I was till in a strange area I did not know, but in a casual way I walked the streets until I saw a sign post I recognized. At my residence no one was surprised that I arrived so late, after all I was thought to be having a good time in the city for the first time.

THE EVENT OF THE
PASSING OF LOWELL JOHNSON

LAST IMPRESSIONS

Lowell Johnson earlier in his life.

 Oratory on Lowell's life would neither suffice nor be seemly, for none of us can claim to stand in judgment against any other. His actions are better known to the Concourse on High than to himself. Nevertheless, he has lived with us on this earthly plane and we are left wondering what the trip there will be like for us or what form it will take.

Only fragments of his life are known by us. We know that he was once a student and behaved as all students did in his day; we know also that he was in WW II ; we also know from the interview he had with Peter Lotis, a Radio Announcer who had worked with him, when he turned ninety, that he had gone to South Africa to study Communications and found himself in the right place at the right time for Baha'i work. Now he has left for the Infinite Worlds of God. He may not have had children of his own, but around the world some have been taught the Faith by him and become his spiritual relatives and children. He nurtured more youths than I have seen anyone do in my time. I remember his excitement when he had taught a young man who was from the Zoroastrian Religion who had become a Baha'i! All these youths are now grown men and women who have remained active in the Faith.

Writing of the right time, reminds me that I know he found me at the right time, after a disappearance of two years, during which time my life had not been quite in conformity with the rule. I had lived by my own limited principles. But at that juncture of meeting him, I was beginning to reassess my life. I wished only for one thing and prayed about it. I wished that, if God had a rockery in the next world, to please accept me as one of the rocks in it. I had found solace in words from the Bible that ran that made feel so humble:

> "For my thoughts are not your thoughts, neither your ways my way, saith the Lord
>
> (Holy Bible, Isaiah 55:8)"

> "10:29. Are not two sparrows sold for a 'farthing? And one of them shall not fall on the ground without your Father
>
> 10:30. But the very hairs of your head are numbered.
>
> 10:31. Fear ye not, therefore, for ye are of more value than many sparrows.
>
> (Holy Bible, Matthew 10)"

This feeling was enhanced when I heard Lowell quote the words of the Creator to Abraham:

> "17:1…the Lord appeared to Abram, and said unto him, I am the Almighty God; walk thou before me , and be thou perfect.
>
> 17:2. And I will make my covenant between me and thee, and will multiply thee exceedingly.
>
> 17:4 As for me, behold , my covenant is with thee, and I shall make thee a father of many nations.
>
> (Holy Bible: Genesis 17)"

I had regarded my search for perfection as being foolish and wasted time. At that moment I felt I had not tried in vain. What was required of me was to find the Law and attempt to obey it as part of a Covenant God had with all humankind.

This period in my life got me started on seeking the Covenant of God, which Lowell Johnson explains in his book: *The Eternal Covenant* (Johnson, 1967)

THE HIDDEN WORDS AND SONG

On his birthday on the 27th April, 2011, and on the 30th of that same month , Lowell was requested to talk at a Baha'i Feast in Johannesburg. He rendered three songs based on words from the Writings of the Faith. One song was about the Greatest Name "Ya Baha'ul Abha" which he pronounced in the old style of the *Star of the West:*

"Ya Baha el Abha"
246 STAR OF THE WEST
- SW, Vol. 12, p. 246

The other two songs are based on the words from the *Hidden Words of Baha'u'llah*

"5. O SON OF BEING!
Love Me, that I may love thee. If thou lovest Me not, My love can in no wise reach thee. Know this, O servant

(Baha'u'llah, The Arabic Hidden Words)"

"1. O SON OF SPIRIT!
My first counsel is this: Possess a pure, kindly and radiant heart, that thine may be a sovereignty ancient, imperishable and everlasting."

(The Arabic Hidden Words)

I was pleasantly surprised to note that, even at the age of ninety one , he could still remember those words off by heart, and be able to sing them in a song. This part is from a video clip taken during the occasion and contributed by Nolitha Mangisa who now serves at the Baha'i World Center.

NAW-RUZ 2012

Lowell spent Naw Ruz visiting with Sarah Ma'ani, an old friend, in Johannesburg. Sarah remembers that day with pleasantness, though she admits, that Lowell's quality of physical life had deteriorated. He seemed to be in good humor. Sarah had started work in South Africa, after pioneering from the United States, helping Lowell in the secretary's office, when Lowell was secretary of the National Spiritual Assembly. I should humbly point out that Lowell helped many lead and appreciate a better quality of spiritual life, a gift that can last forever.

Lowell with Sarah Ma'ani, at Naw-Ruz, 2012 (BE 169).

END DAYS

Lowell was admitted to *Olivedale Clinic* and diagnosed as having a congestive heart failure. He was later discharged to be cared for at home, but soon readmitted with an infection. On discharge the doctors placed him on palliative care with a doctor and nurse in attendance. He soon passed away, on the morning of the 25th May at about 5.00 a.m.. Celia Beaumont kept in touch with all throughout Lowell's sickness.

Thus ended a life of one, who once dreamed of entering a spaceship , without ever remembering leaving it.

ONE WHO WISHED TO TELL A STORY

Marguerite Sears

Earlier, when I was writing some stories about Africa, I found I had to find some authentic sources to clarify some points. I could think of no one nearby who could do this but Marguerite Sears , the wife of the Hand of the Cause William Sears. I wish I had met with her in order to get some stories about all the early believers in Africa, for she lived there and knew them all. She herself, in her letter expressed this wish, but I did not take advantage of it. In a way, I also felt that she was too great a source to approach and I had not thought I would even approach writing a worthy book about my memories of Africa. Writing this simple tale on so great a period in the introduction of the Faith in Africa, I had thought would be the work of others far exalted in station than I. Writing came as an afterthought wherein I plunged foolishly hoping for a mind to read. At that time I had meant to write some few stories on pioneers I met.

Actually, I knew Marguerite through the Hand of the Cause and his *God Loves Laughter*. It was a joy to meet her in person. Once she came to the Baha'i Center in Johannesburg, accompanying her husband who was to meet with Baha'is but had also gone to meet with family. Marguerite carried presents for the Baha'i friends. She had copies a recently released 45 RPM record called "The Queen of Carmel" and was giving each one she met at the Center a copy. That is how I got my copy. I have often marveled at her humility and meekness before others , yet felt the strength of the teacher in her without her having said anything to me. It was through her efforts that the Hand of the Cause met the Faith, yet she remained so meek, resigned and strong for all. It is with great respect that I include her story here. I do this because she wished she could help and in fact offered to assist in any way. I feel her encouragement. This was the third letter she wrote and I never wrote after the one in this book. The book I had meant to write failed to take off at all and it was embarrassing.

Here is Marguerite's letter:

Desert Rose Baha'i School
Marguerite R. Sears
5698 N. Tweedy Rd.
Eloy, AZ 85231
29 June 02.

Dear Robert—

Thank you for the pages you sent. Do you want them back? Wish we could get together to talk about the friends you are writing about: I've a few memories.

About Mike (Sears), He went for 1 1/2 yrs to S.W. Africa

(Namibia) when Ted Kordell was going off for a year to find a wife and Mike didn't want to leave the country empty. There was one African believer at that time. Since then the park where they met is now called "Pioneer Park"!

I have a few things we saved of Mike's—never thinking he'd be gone before me—but thought you might like it—

We are very busy here in spite of the heat—but, at least we're not in the fire area.

I expect to be speaking in Glenwood Falls, Colo. For the Anniversary of Abdu'l-Baha's visit there—-the theme is "memories"—so S. Africa will have a big place in my talk—

Baha'i love,

Marguerite.

PTO

Yesterday I was surprised, in a store, to see a lady wearing a Basuto straw hat. I went up to talk with her and asked where she was from in Lesotho. "Michigan", she answered—-my aunt brought this from there——

Ah well—-M

I could tell that Marguerite was really interested in writing some stories about Africa. But, due to misunderstandings and software challenges on both sides of the sea—for, initially a book was to be published in Africa—the writing of that book could not progress. Even though Marguerite supplied me with her telephone number and email address I was to embarrassed to even contact her anymore on the matter. Finally I intimated the failure of the book to Lowell, who felt I was starting off all on the wrong step. He advised that I do not write about the pioneers, but that, instead I should list all the important years of life and write a story on each area. Thus my first book became an autobiography.

I leave the story of writing about Marguerite to others more equipped, for, even though I knew her as a great teacher and a good mother to many, I do not know her beginnings as well as I should. I hope for this she herself will find forgiveness for me and pray that I acquit myself as a worthy Baha'i in His sight, so that I am not shamefaced on the day of my departure for the Worlds Beyond this. Here I wish to mention her ardent encouragement and her wish to assist by telling some stories herself. Perhaps, had I visited and listened to her story, my time would have been spent in writing more in depth about early believers in Africa. I failed to do this , through shyness and short-sightedness of its import.

A REFLECTION

A nucleus takes much to build, especially putting up a structure that had not existed before. To some it seems to border on Utopia to even think of a united world, but to Baha'is this is not just a possibility but a structure under construction. The Baha'i Faith started with one man in the far away Shiraz of Persia, who received the news of a New Day, and in 169 years this Faith has embraced all the worlds courtiers in existence and its adherents number in the millions. The number grows all the time..

The Baha'is have to present a model to the world, a model of a world community that actually functions in peace , and is not established upon the shedding of blood , except that blood that the sacrifices the Baha'is make in establishing the Faith, is shed in the path of service. The Baha'is plead with the world to accept this model as it is not manmade, but is part of a divine plan for humankind. However, whether the world in general accepts the plan in the immediate future or not, the Baha'is will continue to execute their peaceful plan, until it is noticed by all.

It may sound audacious and assumptive for them to attempt, this but they are in obedience to a command of One Who spent over forty years in prison, and Who bore a Message of unity and peace for all, from on High. The important thing is not to accept this as a bare statement but to investigate it with justice and without fear of losing ones self in the Truth. The fear of losing identity has ever been a cause of many a pain and attempted purging amongst us, but this has been and will continue to be, self-defeating, as 'all things are involved in all things'. The source and beginning of humankind is one and has been one and undivided through time.

The model created by Baha'is now exists and it is up to mankind to turn to a plan, not of their own creating, but a plan that is founded on the promises of the Eternal which stand visible in all the Holy Books. The Baha'i Faith is democratic in its institutions but it is devoid of all political parties (Michael Sears, 1977)

It has been asserted that anger is part of the emotions that characterize humans, and from this standpoint, it has been concluded that war is part and parcel of human existence and predisposes man to want to fight. The Baha'i Faith has proved that progress towards unity can be achieved without the shedding of blood. Baha'is number in the millions and exist in many countries by sacrificing their lives in the teaching field.

It has also been suggested that war is a method of controlling populations. This is very strange, for earthquakes and other cataclysms achieve this with no assistance from man. Albeit, if we say that this is waste, then we have to claim that this life is all there is and that beyond that there is nothing. If man ever fears death, man will live in a state of apprehension, but if man believes in eternal perpetuation of life, then man will live in hope , and hope is ever an enemy of anxiety. If we endorse eternal existence, then we can easily endorse the belief or assertion of the General Systems Theory, mainly that a system never dies but continues existing in one form or another (Skyttner p. 43). Again, sameness of type is not possible, as by procreation, uniqueness of type is exponential. Even Siamese twins may have divergent interests in life. Therefore, we cannot achieve our non-existence by declaring ourselves to be no more than a repetition of the same carbon copies.

It is a tautology to say that all animals are animals, but this does not apply to humans. Animals obey the rules of nature, consistently. Man's behavior is conditioned by values. The acquisition of values falls within the realm of the will and curiosity of humankind, but similar values may not be an intrinsic descriptions of all, as they need to be acquired. Though anger occurs naturally in everyone, each has the responsibility of curbing and living above animalistic instincts. Man rules nature, not the other way around.

Those who are and have labored in the building of the Kingdom, find encouragement in these words from the Writings of Baha'u'llah

"Happy the days that have been consecrated to the remembrance of God and blessed the hours which have been spent in praise of Him Who is the All-Wise. By My life! Neither the pomp of the mighty, nor the wealth of the rich, nor even the ascendancy of the ungodly will endure. All will perish, at a word from Him. He, verily, is the All-Powerful, the All-Compelling, the Almighty"

(Baha'u'llah, Gleanings from the
Writings of Baha'u'llah, p. 138)

"2232. Blessed is he who in the prime of his youth and the heyday of his life will arise to serve the Cause of the Lord of the beginning and of the end, and adorn his heart with His love. The manifestation of such a grace is greater than the creation of the heavens and of the earth. Blessed are the steadfast and well is it with those who are firm. (From a Tablet - translated from the Persian)"

(The Compilation of Compilations vol. II, p. 415)

A QUOTE FROM THE WRITINGS OF BAHA'U'LLAH:

The Great Being saith: O well-beloved ones! The tabernacle of unity hath been raised; regard ye not one another as strangers. Ye are the fruits of one tree, and the leaves of one branch. We cherish the hope that the light of justice may shine upon the world and sanctify it from tyranny

(Gleanings from the Writings of Baha'u'llah, p. 218)

GLOSSARY

'Abdu'l-Baha: The title of Abbas Effendi , eldest son of Baha'u'llah, the prophet of the Baha'i Faith, Whom He appointed as the Center of His Covenant, after His Passing , to prevent schism amongst the Baha'is. The English meaning of the title is "Servant of Baha".

Apartheid: A system of government used in South African, and based on White Superiority. In a sense, it was an oligarchy system, of a few ruling the many.

Bab: A Gate. The name of the Forerunner who announced the coming of Baha'u'llah in 1844

Baha: Splendour

Baha'i: A follower of the Baha'i Faith

Baha'i Faith: A religion founded in 1863 by Mirza Husayn Ali, later was called Baha'u'llah.

Baha'u'llah: A title that means "The Splendour of God", and refers to the Prophet of the Baha'i Faith

Bantu Education: A South African educational system planned by the Apartheid government for Africans only. It was deplored by all educated Africans

Circumcision: A custom observed amongst Xhosas and signifies initiation into manhood. It is performed after a boy has gone through puberty.

Counsellor: A member of the Continental Board of Counsellors. This Board is appointed from Baha'is of different continents by the Universal House and is intended to help continue some of the duties of the Hands of the Cause. Both men and women may be appointed to this service.

Greatest Name: This is the greeting of Baha'is: "Allah'u'Abha" (God is Most Glorious) or an invocation "Ya Baha'u'l' Abha" (O Thou the Glory of the Most Glorious), used by Baha'is.

Group Areas Act: This was an act in South Africa whereby all race groups were to settle each in a separate area delimited by the government.

Guardian: The title "the Guardian of the Faith of Baha'u'llah" refers to Shoghi Effendi, who was appointed to the position by his Grandfather, 'Abdu'l-Baha

Hands of the Cause: These were certain Baha'is who had been given important duties by Baha'u'llah, 'Abdu'l-Baha and Shoghi Effendi. In recent times there were Twenty seven, nine of whom resided in Haifa, Israel. The rest travelled teaching throughout the world. They have all passed on.

Influx Control Office: This office controlled the flow of Africans into and out of the cities.

Kitab-i-Iqan: or Book of Certitude: This is a book revealed by Baha'u'llah in two days and two nights while He resided in Baghdad. It explains the scriptures of the past and the present and how they are related.

Local Spiritual Assembly: A body of nine adult Baha'is, in a local community, elected, annually at Ridvan by Baha'is of mature age, through private ballots, and who form the administration for that locality. Local Spiritual Assemblies are designated as Primary Houses of Justice

National Spiritual Assembly: A body of nine adult Baha'is elected by delegates from localities, when the delegates meet annually during Ridvan at a National Convention. Voting is by secret ballot and there is no lobbying. The duties of a National Assembly include attending to national and individual needs of Baha'is. National Spiritual Assemblies are designated as Secondary Houses of Justice.

Necklace treatment: A method of execution used in South Africa during the riots in the eighties , where one suspected of being a government informer, had a rubber tire forced onto the shoulders, is drenched with gasoline and set alight.

Nomonde: A Xhosa name given to a girl or woman and means "mother of patient care"

Obligatory Prayers: There are three obligatory prayers in the Baha'i Faith and each Bahia has to choose one of them to say on daily basis and in the prescribed manner.

Pilgrimage: A religious observance that involves visiting holy places of that religion. To go on pilgrimage, a Baha'i has to make an application for permission to visit.

Reference Book: A document in the form of a booklet, carried by all Africans in South Africa, during the Apartheid System, in which details of employment, residence, payment of tax, as well as registration to work in any area, were recorded. This booklet had to be on one's person at all times, and any policemen could demand one to produce it. Failure entailed a fine or a jail sentence.

Ridvan: A holy period, amongst Baha'is, when they elect their administrative bodies. It commemorates a period during which Baha'u'llah, their Prophet, declared His Mission outside Baghdad, at the Garden of Ridvan; between April 21st and May 2nd in 1863, when He was being banished to Constantinople

Sour milk: Milk kept in a container until it sours .It is then used for meals by African in some areas of South Africa. In olden times, such milk was kept in leather containers.

Staff Room: A room reserved in a school for teachers only, which they use for breaks and for change of classes.

Universal House of Justice: An international, administrative Baha'i Body of nine men elected every five years at an International Convention ,by National Assemblies of the Baha'i world. This election is in essence the same as the elections of the other administrative bodies, however, the decisions of the Universal House, after it has been formed, are infallible. The nine members of the Universal House of Justice reside in Haifa, Israel throughout their term of service, leaving only for short periods to teach or visit.

Vigilantes: men employed by the South African government and imported from out of the cities to be on patrol duty in African townships and charged to keep order. They were generally violent in this task.

REFERENCES

Baha'i Faith(1991). *Baha'i Prayers.* Wilmette, IL: Baha'i Publishing Trust.

Baha'i Faith.(1976). *Baha'i World Faith.* Wilmette, IL: Baha'i Publishing Trust.

Baha'i Faith (1979). *Epistle to the Son of the Wolf.* Wilmette, IL: Baha'i Publishing Trust.

Baha'i Faith(1952). *Gleanings from the writings of Baha'u'llah.* Wilmette, IL: Baha'i Publishing Trust.

Baha'i Faith.(1960). *Kitab-i-Iqan.* Wilmette, IL.: Baha'i Publishing Trust.

Baha'i Faith(1991). *The compilation of compilations vol. II.* Maryborough, Australia: Baha'i Publications Australia.

Baha'i Faith.(1980). *The Hidden Words of Baha'u'llah.* Wilmette, IL: Baha'i Publishing Trust

Holy Bible: Authorized King James Version. London, U.K. Oxford University Press.

Sears, M.(1977) *A democracy without politics.* A talk delivered at the Baha'i National Center, Johannesburg, South Africa.

Sears, W.(1985) *All Flags Flying.* Johannesburg, South Africa: National Spiritual Assembly of the Baha'is of South and West Africa.

Shoghi Effendi(1970), *The Dawn-Breakers; Nabil's Narrative of the Early days of the Baha'i Revelation (Translated)..* Wilmette, IL: Baha'i Publishing Trust.

Skyttner, L.(2005). *General systems theory.* Singapore: World Scientific Publishing Co. Pte. Ltd.

Taherzadeh, A.(2001) *The revelation of Baha'u'llah Vol. I.* Kidlington, Oxford: George Ronald, Publisher.